FREE TO FLY
DARE TO BE A SUCCESS

by
Helene Rothschild
and
Marsha Kay Seff

Published by
R & E PUBLISHERS
P. O. Box 2008
Saratoga, California 95070

Library of Congress Card Catalog Number
85-62441

I.S.B.N.
0-88247-748-X

Dedicated to your inner peace,

the greatest contribution you can make

towards world peace

ACKNOWLEDGEMENTS

I would like to express my deepest appreciation to the following people:

My clients, for your courage to face your fears; for trusting me to help you heal yourself; and for all that you have taught me as we journeyed together on your growth path.

Specifically, the nine clients quoted in this book who were courageously willing to share their personal stories in order to help others.

My mother and father, for encouraging me to be an independent thinker; for supporting me in my goals and for teaching me how to play.

My beautiful daughters, Karen and Deborah, for your love and the patience you showed me — your busy, professional mother.

My friends and interns for hearing and believing in me.

My many teachers who are too numerous to mention separately. They include: my professors, workshop facilitators, lecturers, and authors.

My co-author, Marsha Kay Seff, for allowing your skepticism to change to acceptance and excitement as you studied the theory of Creative Therapy and began using it in your own growth process. And for your hard work and loyal commitment to helping me write this book so that I can share what I have learned with the world!

Love,

Helene Rothschild

v

TABLE OF CONTENTS

PART III
THE TOOLS

PART I
Fear of Success

Chapter 1

The Ropes That Bind

Marriage means living in a birdcage — at least that's how it felt to Jack and me during the 12 years we spent together. Marriage was the cage, and we were the trapped little birds who didn't have the chance to fly free. No wonder after that experience, whenever I began to get close to another man, I panicked and flew to safer ground.

Jack and I came from a generation that believed that men and women were bound by two different sets of responsibilities. I, as wife and mother, was expected to stay home and tend the family, while Jack, as husband and father, worked to support us.

On the rare evenings that we went out together, I was responsible for finding a babysitter. I also did all the shopping, including picking out Jack's clothes. Once, I remember, when I threw out his ratty old jacket, he refused to shop for another. Then when he caught a cold, he blamed it on me.

We usually did what he wanted and when he wanted to do it. When it came to me, he was jealous and over-protective. He wouldn't let me have any male friends; he wouldn't even allow me to play tennis with a man. "If you really love me, Helene," Jack would shout, "you'll do what I say."

I did love him, and for a long time I did exactly what he said. Like him, I'd also bought the unwritten rule about the woman taking care of her man.

But I grew increasingly more angry and resentful. And when the inevitable divorce freed me, I felt like a bird that had finally escaped from her cage. I can remember running down the beach one day with my arms outstretched, yelling, "I'm free. I'm free to fly."

I promised myself that day that I would never again be locked up. And I remained single for eight years.

During most of that time, I was lonely and desperately wanted a

1

special man in my life. But I managed to sabotage one chance of success after another.

I wouldn't allow myself to succeed in a loving relationship, because I didn't want to give up my newly discovered freedom. To me, marriage meant returning to the dreaded birdcage.

Does my story sound familiar? Although each of us is unique, our problems are not.

We all can allow ourselves to be locked up in cages of one sort or another. And while we may long to be free, we often act as our own jailers.

Take a close look at yourself. Are you happy with who you are and what you're doing? Are you in a fulfilling relationship? Are you reaching your career goals?

If not, why not? What's keeping you from achieving the success and happiness you want and deserve?

As strange as it may sound, nobody but you. If you're not getting what you want out of life, no matter how hard you try, you can probably blame it on fear. Not fear of failure but, crazy as it seems, Fear of Success.

In this technological world, where all kinds of wonderful opportunities are within our reach, Fear of Success has become a universal plague. It's so widespread, in fact, that it may be considered the norm. I believe that almost everyone of us suffers from a certain degree of Fear of Success in at least one area of our lives.

By success, I don't mean the popular definition: Being the top man or woman on the totem pole or having lots of money. Success is more than that. To be successful, you have to *feel* successful.

Unfortunately, many of us are under the misconception that success is something that can be measured by dollar signs on a bank account, by the number of job promotions or by a wedding album on the coffee table. We have been taught that success is an external achievement. We think it's a list of accomplishments, things that others can give to us.

We say, "If only I get that new job or position or that big contract, then I'll be successful. If only that person will marry me, then I'll be happy." When we get the job or the special someone, our happiness is short-lived. Soon, we're miserable again, empty inside.

I have clients who are married, earn $50,000-plus a year, and hold positions of power and influence. In the eyes of most people, they're very successful. So, why aren't they happy?

They're not happy because they don't *feel* successful. They've learned the hard way that success isn't out there, that nobody else can give it to us. Success isn't determined by the standards of the rest of the world; it's something that we experience inside. As I see it, *true success is an internal feeling of fulfillment, peace and power which comes from being who we really are and doing what we truly want to do.*

We are the only ones who can feel our joy or our pain, and we are the only ones who can feel our success. But we can only experience that success when we are able to overcome the fears that are sabotaging us.

Nobody ever comes to therapy claiming to be afraid of success. Some of you already may be shaking your head, denying that you have such a fear. Instead, you claim it's the possibility of failing that scares you. Well, on the conscious level, that might be true.

But unlike fear of failure, which is easy to recognize, Fear of Success is subconscious. It's often hidden underneath fear of failure.

For example, you may be thinking, "I don't want to try another relationship, because I'm afraid I will fail again." If you explore further, you may discover that you're also feeling, "I don't deserve to be happy."

Another example of fear of failure is "I can't take that promotion, because I'm not smart enough." Buried beneath that may be the Fear of Success: "Being a manager doesn't fit my image of myself."

It is these subconscious fears that hurt us the most, the invisible obstacles that keep tripping us when we try to move forward.

In order to move on, we first have to recognize the symptoms of self-sabotage and then work on the real causes. Picture yourself as a tree whose branches are weak and dying. These unhealthy branches represent your painful relationships, unhappiness in your career, depression, poor health, alcoholism or obesity.

The reasons for these symptoms, the real causes of your unhappiness, are in the roots of the tree. The frustrating problems in your life are symptoms indicating that you have, in your roots, negative thoughts that are running your life. You have made the unconscious decision, "I'm not OK, I don't deserve happiness, I'm ugly, I'm worthless, I'm unimportant, I'm unlovable, I'm dumb or I'm not enough." Only by uncovering and treating these roots of your unhappiness, your self-defeating fears, can you have healthy branches, or positive symptoms, like successful careers, fulfilling relationships and healthy, attractive bodies.

I discovered Fear of Success with my very first client. Betty felt like a failure in her relationships with men. "If only the right man would ask me to marry him," she would say. But she never seemed able to create that right man in her life.

I sensed that the answer to her problem was in her subconscious,

3

The Basis of Creative Therapy

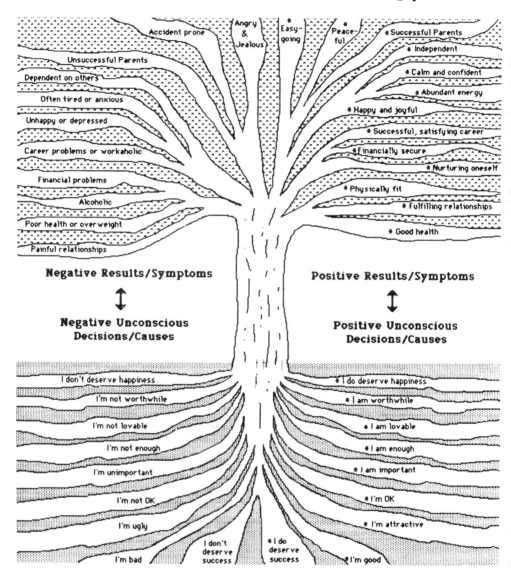

Accident prone Angry & Jealous *Easy-going *Peaceful *Successful Parents

Unsuccessful Parents
Dependent on others
Often tired or anxious
Unhappy or depressed
Career problems or workaholic
Financial problems
Alcoholic
Poor health or overweight
Painful relationships

*Independent
*Calm and confident
*Abundant energy
*Happy and joyful
*Successful, satisfying career
*Financially secure
*Nurturing oneself
*Physically fit
*Fulfilling relationships
*Good health

Negative Results/Symptoms

↕

**Negative Unconscious
Decisions/Causes**

Positive Results/Symptoms

↕

**Positive Unconscious
Decisions/Causes**

I don't deserve happiness
I'm not worthwhile
I'm not lovable
I'm not enough
I'm unimportant
I'm not OK
I'm ugly
I don't deserve success
I'm bad

*I do deserve happiness
*I am worthwhile
*I am lovable
*I am enough
*I am important
*I'm OK
*I'm attractive
*I do deserve success
*I'm good

4

and asked Betty to close her eyes and picture the right man asking her to marry him.

"How do you feel?" I asked.

"Terrified," she answered.

There is was, the insidious fear. On the conscious level, Betty wanted marriage. But underneath that, on a subconscious level, she was afraid of getting what she wanted. Though she didn't realize it at the time, she was allowing all kinds of imaginary ropes to hold her back. Only when she became aware of her fears and broke through them, was she able to reach her goal.

And Betty's story certainly wasn't unique. As I worked with a succession of clients, I continued to see this Fear of Success. I never heard those exact words, but the same feelings and fears were frequently there. Virtually everytime I asked clients to picture themselves having what they wanted or being who they wanted to be, they said they felt scared. When I asked what was frightening them, most of them had similar answers. A pattern emerged, and I began to categorize the most prevalent blocks to success.

It was like each one of my clients was being held back by strong ropes. Picture yourself floating above the city in a hot air balloon still tied to the ground. Only by cutting the ropes can you soar to the destination of your dreams.

That goes for every form of success, from finding love and striking it rich to losing weight and enjoying good health. Only when you feel lovable will you succeed in a relationship. Only by believing you deserve wealth will you allow yourself to make money and enjoy it. And only by eliminating your need to punish yourself will you let yourself be attractive, healthy and happy.

The way I see it, each one of us could take off in our own hot air balloon to create what we want in our lives, if only we weren't bound by the seven ropes I call The Seven Fears of Success. Some of us are held down by all of them; others by only a few.

Briefly, here are The Seven Fears of Success:

1. Fear of the unknown. "I'm afraid to find out what it would be like to be thin and gorgeous."

2. Fear that success does not fit my image of myself. "What's a truck driver's son like me doing in an ivy league college?"

3. Fear that I don't deserve success. "I once stole money."

4. Fear that people will not like me if I'm successful. "Everyone knows that most men are intimidated by successful women."

5. Fear that success has some scary consequences, that it will make me vulnerable, cut into my free time or result in greater responsibility. "If I fall in love again, I will have to give up my freedom and return to my cage."

6. Fear that my parents won't love me if I'm more successful than they. "I don't want my father to think that I could make more money than he."

7. Fear that to be successful is to fulfill my parents' wishes, and I'm angry at them. "I'll show them, I'm not going to be a successful doctor."

The purpose of this book is to help you learn to identify the ropes that are holding you back and then give you the tools to cut them. The checklist in the next chapter can help you more specifically identify some of your hidden fears. Then, in the last few chapters, there are more than 30 exercises and 150 affirmations that will show you how to move beyond your Fear of Success so that you can create what you want in all aspects of your life.

Chapter 2 _____

Will You Allow Yourself to Succeed?

To find out if you're stopping yourself from getting what you want in your personal and professional life, read the following statements. Check off the ones in each category that apply directly to you. It's best to move through the list quickly, putting down your first response.

Life in General

_____I don't deserve to be happy.
_____I don't think of myself as lovable.
_____I will lose my friends if I'm too successful.
_____I am afraid of the responsibility of a relationship or a career.
_____I wouldn't feel right being more successful than my parents.
_____I stay in an unpleasant job or relationship because it's familiar.
_____I resent the fact that my parents push me to succeed.
_____It scares me to get what I want.
_____I feel guilty when I'm too happy.
_____As soon as things start going well, something bad always happens.
_____I have trouble accepting compliments.
_____People notice me only when I make mistakes or need help.
_____I get a stomach ache when I picture myself getting what I want.
_____I'm dumb.
_____I'm not enough.
_____I'm worthless.
_____I'm not important.
_____I'm not O.K.
_____No man wants a successful career woman.
_____When people ask me to do things, I can't say no.

Career

_____ I can't decide what kind of job I want.

_____ I'm a procrastinator.

_____ I'm afraid to be more successful than my husband.

_____ If I'm successful, I will not have enough time to spend with my family or do the things I like to do.

_____ Famous people don't have private lives.

_____ I'm afraid of burn-out.

_____ If I make it to the top, I can fall harder and farther.

_____ Women and other minorities don't have a chance to succeed in certain fields.

_____ Success means power, and power corrupts.

_____ If I make too much money, I'll have to pay too much in taxes.

Money

_____ Money is the root of all evil.

_____ Rich people are mean and greedy.

_____ Money changes people.

_____ I can't imagine myself prosperous.

_____ Making money is a struggle.

_____ I feel guilty about spending money.

_____ I don't deserve more money.

_____ If I were rich, I'd be expected to take care of others.

_____ If I had lots of money, I'd have to worry about people stealing it.

_____ Money is too much of a responsibility.

_____ I'm irresponsible with money.

Relationships

_____ Relationships are demanding and too time-consuming.

_____ In a relationship, you have to think of the other person to the exclusion of yourself.

_____ Marriage is too much of a responsibility.

_____ I only like one-night stands.

_____ Every relationship means a permanent commitment.

_____ I can't handle both a successful career and a relationship.

_____ There's no one out there for me.

_____ I will get hurt again if I let myself be vulnerable.

_____ If I let people really get to know me, they won't like me.

_____ I'm ugly and unlovable.

_____Since I walked out of my last relationship, I don't deserve to be happy.

_____People I love leave me.

Sex

_____People want me only for sex.

_____If I'm sexual with someone, that person will expect a permanent commitment.

_____I feel too vulnerable when I'm sexual.

_____I resent having to perform for my sexual partner.

_____I feel pressured to have an orgasm to please my partner.

_____I feel guilty about enjoying my sexuality.

_____If I initiate sex, my partner will think I'm too aggressive.

_____If I enjoy sex too much, men will think I'm loose.

_____I'm afraid that the more sex I have, the more I will want.

Weight

_____No matter how hard I try, I can't lose weight.

_____When I lose weight, I just gain it right back.

_____I feel safer when I'm overweight.

_____When my body started to develop, people teased me.

_____I feel weak when I'm thin.

_____The last time I was thin, I was sick.

_____Food was scarce when I was a child, and I'm still afraid of being hungry.

_____My best times with my family were at the dinner table.

_____I'm not going to lose weight as long as my spouse or parents nag me about it.

_____When I'm fat, I don't have to worry about dating.

_____I'm afraid that when I'm thin and attractive, I won't be able to resist sexual advances.

_____If I'm thin, people will only want me for my body.

_____I find myself overeating when things start going well.

Sports/Talent/Health

_____If I do well in sports, people will think I'm dumb.

_____Men don't like women to beat them at sports.

_____I can't imagine myself as a winner.

_____I avoid doing things that my parents or siblings do well.

9

_____You can't make a living being an artist or musician.

_____I've always been unhealthy.

_____I get lots of attention when I'm ill or hurt.

_____I often have accidents or hurt myself when things start going well.

_____When I'm sick, I can give up many of my responsibilities.

_____At least when I'm sick, I can stay home and relax.

_____I deserve to suffer.

Well, how many checks do you have? At one time or another, I've heard everyone of these statements from either my clients, friends, or myself. If you checked off even one, you could be suffering from Fear of Success.

10

Chapter 3 _____

Rooting Out The Seven Fears

You may be as surprised as my clients and I were to uncover some of your feelings about success. Like most of us, you probably think you're too mature to be afraid of many of these things. Well, chances are you're right.

But I found out that we don't make such decisions as intelligent, worldly adults. We make them when we're very young, basing them on limited experience and information. Often, by the time we're 5 years old (for some people, 7 or 8), we jump to false conclusions.

As children, we believe the whole world revolves around us. So we feel responsible for everything that happens. We're like mathematicians, constantly making equations:

Daddy never plays with me = I'm not important.
Mommy always criticizes me = I'm a bad person.
My parents always fight = I'm responsible for their problems, so I must be a terrible person.
My Daddy left us = I must be unlovable.
My teachers don't listen to me = I'm worthless.
Other kids tease me = I'm not enough.
I come from a poor, black family = Being a doctor doesn't fit my image of myself.

The examples are endless. However unintentionally it happens, children pick up on the wrong information and believe it. Even as adults, we continue to hear—and act on—these negative thoughts that cause us pain and frustration. Long after we're old enough to know better, we allow the negative and incorrect decisions of our childhood to rule our lives and keep us from succeeding.

When we feel that we're not okay, that we don't deserve good things, we sabotage ourselves by attracting people into our lives who will reinforce our worthlessness. We sabotage ourselves in all sorts of ingenious-but-unconscious ways. We push away things that we want and find excuses for not getting them. We're offered a job, and we find a long list of reasons for not taking it. We say things like, "I can't handle the responsibility. I don't have enough experience. I'm not smart enough. The company isn't right for me."

Or we take the job and prove these fears through our behavior. We come late to work, make unnecessary mistakes, procrastinate or pick fights with our boss and colleagues. We may even get sick or have an accident.

We sabotage our relationships in similar ways. We meet someone special and we start getting close. Suddenly, we begin finding fault with each other. "She's too loud; he's too short." We become demanding and start arguments. We make commitments and we break them. We push away our special friends or we create people in our lives who will push us away. Our fears become self-fulfilling prophesies.

When we don't get what we think we want, we're quick to blame others. Or we run away from our fears by focusing our energies instead on a single aspect of our lives—our work, children, hobbies, or even alcohol or drugs.

Obviously, some of these escapes are more acceptable than others, but none of them works indefinitely. Consider the workaholic who puts all his time into his business and then is devastated when his wife leaves him.

In the long run, we hurt ourselves. We push away people who love us, fail in a career for which we are well-suited, or give up and get sick—all because we're afraid.

The truth is that there's nothing wrong with being afraid. We're all afraid sometimes. Welcome to the human race!

We need fear in order to survive—it keeps us from carelessly crossing a busy street or speeding on a treacherous mountain road. But we don't need fear to hold us back or paralyze us when, in reality, it's safe to move.

To cross that street, to move beyond your Fear of Success to where you want to be, you need to go inside your subconscious.

In order to change your feelings about success and consequently your thinking, I have found that you first have to be able to "see" the original, hurtful experiences that made you feel the way you do. Just talking about your problems isn't enough.

"Close your eyes," I tell my clients, "and see clearly." By closing your eyes, you can block out your present circumstances and go back to the root of your problems.

I use visualization, or guided imagery, to help clients return to the time they as children made their original negative decisions. These decisions are like tapes recorded in our subconscious, and we play them over and over again.

After you get in touch with the pain they are causing, you have to release it in a safe, supportive environment. If you're sad, you need to cry. If you're scared, you have to acknowledge and experience your fear. The same goes for anger.

This is an important step. Before you can take in positive feelings, you have to eliminate the trauma of the negative ones. Picture a tall glass filled with dirt, or negative thoughts. Before you can fill that glass with fresh, clean water, with positive decisions, you have to empty out the dirt. Otherwise, you'll just get mud.

In order to make these positive decisions, you need positive experiences. That's where the *creative* part of the therapy comes in. With your eyes closed, you visualize new experiences in place of the old ones. For example, instead of your father being too busy for you, you see him spending lots of time with you. As a result, you're free to make a new, positive equation: "He is spending time with me = I am important."

The final step is reinforcing this new decision with a positive statement, an affirmation which you repeat regularly to yourself. "I, Helene, am important."

My process may sound illogical to some people, but it does work. These techniques have helped hundreds of my clients find success in a relatively short period of time.

As a licensed marriage, family, and child therapist, I developed this process I call Creative Therapy using my own creative tools and theories in combination with those from Gestalt, Psychosynthesis, Behaviorism, Transactional Analysis, Biofeedback, and Bioenergetics. I also integrated some theories of Freud, Jung, Rogers, and Satir.

The therapy that evolved proved so successful in helping people, that I soon had more clients than I could work with alone. As a result, I founded the Institute for Creative Therapy, a non-profit, educational center in California, and began training other therapists to use my techniques. It has worked out so well that I envision someday setting up a worldwide network of Creative Therapy institutes.

Meantime, I've taught my techniques for overcoming Fear of Success at more than 200 lectures, seminars and workshops. And on my own cable-TV show, I've actually counseled clients on camera. I have also appeared on many other television and radio talkshows, and produced a cassette tape, *Breaking Through Fear of Success*.

13

One of the exciting benefits of this therapy is that the lay person can learn to use many of the tools to help himself. Let's take a look at each of the Seven Fears of Success to see the different ways the process can work.

1. FEAR OF THE UNKNOWN

For some reason, we humans are afraid of the unknown, things we've never seen or done before. We'll stay in a miserable job or an unhappy relationship simply because we already know what it's like. No matter how bad, at least it's familiar. We don't know what will happen if we take a chance on change. We would rather be safe than satisfied!

My client Bill was one of these people. He came to me complaining that he hated his job, but he was afraid to give it up to find something else.

I asked Bill to close his eyes and see himself many years from now, still working at the same desk. What he saw was an unhappy, tired man.

"What do you want to say to that man?" I asked.

"I wish you had left that miserable job and done what you really wanted years ago," was the answer.

"What do you want to do now?" I asked.

"I want to leave my job to start another career, and I'm going to do just that!"

"Even though you're scared?"

"Yes," Bill said in a calm and certain voice. "Even though I'm scared."

Often, we have to be in an enormous amount of pain before we're willing to move on. Sometimes, a death of a loved one, a divorce, a birthday, or a severe illness shakes us up enough to give us the push we need.

At that point, we may decide that we have suffered enough; that we're not going to spend the rest of our lives in pain. That's when we start to grow, take risks and create what we want in our lives. That's when we're ready to make the commitment to feel good and be happy.

But each one of us has to make that commitment to ourselves; no one else is powerful enough to do it for us. We need to say, "I'm tired of suffering. I'm ready to move on, even though I am scared of the unknown. Success and happiness are what I really want."

2. SUCCESS DOESN'T FIT MY IMAGE OF MYSELF

For better or worse, we all strive to live up to the image we have of ourselves. If our image is a good one, we do well; if it's a negative one, we can hurt ourselves. If our self-image is that of an employee, for example, we will not allow ourselves to become a manager. It just doesn't fit our image. If we see ourselves as unlovable, we'll push away the people who tell us that we're lovable. If we see ourselves as poor, we'll sabotage our financial success.

Take me, for instance. Although I wanted to join a posh local tennis club last year and could well afford it, something kept me from filling out the application. "I'd better save the money for something more important. I don't play well enough. And I won't fit in anyway." For a time, I continued to sabotage myself with this thinking, although none of it was true.

It was a classic Fear of Success. You see, being a member of a high-priced tennis club didn't fit my image of myself as a poor girl from Brooklyn, New York. My subconscious wouldn't allow a poor New Yorker in an exclusive California club.

Unless I worked on changing the "poor girl" image, I knew that I would continue to find ways of sabotaging my membership. So, I went to work on updating that image, visualizing myself as a successful therapist who could certainly afford the membership. I did eventually join, and I'm having a wonderful time (although I'm still not ready for Wimbledon). I broke through the fear that success didn't fit my image; and as soon as I did, I was able to be successful —allow myself to do what I really wanted.

3. FEAR THAT I DON'T DESERVE SUCCESS

Nobody is harder on us than we are on ourselves. So many of us feel guilty about something we once did or avoided doing.

Guilt is a dangerous feeling to hold onto. We must learn to forgive ourselves for whatever is making us feel bad. If we continue nurturing our guilt, we will punish ourselves by not allowing ourselves to be happy and successful. And while we punish ourselves, we're also hurting the people around us. We need to say we are sorry, forgive ourselves, and then let go of it.

Joan came to me because she wasn't happy with the way her career was going. I asked her to say, "I can't be successful because . . . ." and finish the statement.

"I can't be successful because I'm bad," she answered.

We went back to the time when she originally made that decision. She saw herself at 10 years old, stealing money from her parent's cash register. At 50 years old, Joan was still punishing herself for something she did as a child.

I asked her to imagine that she was 10 years old again, standing in front of her parents. She had to finish that unfinished business, tell her parents what she needed to tell them.

"Mom and Dad," she responded, "I stole money from your

cash register, and I'm very sorry about it. Please forgive me."

She saw her parents forgive her, and she was finally able to forgive herself. She reinforced her new decision by making an affirmation: "I, Joan, am a good person and I deserve success."

"Wow," Joan admitted at the end of that session, "I feel lighter. I've been carrying around that burden for a long time."

And we do. We can feel guilty about something no matter how long ago it happened; adult guilts often reinforce the ones we take with us from childhood. We carry around all this unnecessary baggage until we become aware of it and learn to let go.

4. FEAR THAT PEOPLE WILL NOT LIKE ME IF I'M SUCCESSFUL

This is a very common fear. Women learn early not to be too intelligent lest they scare men away. Similar fears often start in grade school when, for instance, an exceptionally smart student is taunted by peers. The child learns early that to be successful means to invite ridicule. So he may start sabotaging himself, purposely neglecting homework and flunking tests. Before long, his subconscious takes over, and as an adult he continues to hold himself back in hopes that people will like him.

When Lynn came to one of my success workshops, she was concerned that she wasn't going anywhere in her job. It seemed that everytime she was up for a promotion, something got in her way.

I asked her to close her eyes and imagine herself getting the promotion. "How do you feel?" I asked.

"Scared!"

I asked what was scaring her, and she said, "I'm afraid that my husband will be hurt and jealous if I make more money than he does."

I suggested that she discuss her fears with her husband. When she did, she discovered that he was very proud of her accomplishments and would be delighted with her promotion.

The fear that people will not like us if we're successful can stop us in any area of our lives. I'm sure you've heard statements like these: "My friends will think I'm conceited if I tell them about my successes. People won't play with me if I'm too good. My co-workers will resent me if I get the promotion."

So, even when we accomplish what we have dreamed about—win a round of golf or tie up an important business deal—we attempt to downplay it. "I just got lucky. Yes, I succeeded at that, but I didn't get this."

We hold ourselves back from reaching our true potential because we're afraid that it will hurt other people; ironically, we often end up hurting them as well as ourselves. That's because when we inhibit ourselves, we tend to feel angry and resentful. And those feelings can destroy our relationships.

In reality, some people will resent our success because they're frustrated themselves. We need to understand that and move on to friends and lovers who will reinforce our accomplishments.

And we, in turn, can support their achievements. When we're successful, we provide a model for our friends and lovers. "Look at me, I did it and so can you!" Our success is a gift we give to those around us.

5. FEAR THAT SUCCESS HAS FRIGHTENING CONSEQUENCES

Although many people claim that they want to succeed, they don't want the worry and responsibility that they believe go with success. They're afraid that if they're successful, they won't have enough free time for themselves or their families or, worse, that they'll be overwhelmed with work and burn out. Or they feel that success will make them vulnerable.

These negative beliefs are not inherent in success. But as long as we believe them, we will surely avoid our goals. I used to sing, "I've got plenty of nothing and nothing to worry about." And I wondered why I wasn't creating money in my life!

As a child, I believed that rich people spent a lot of time worrying about protecting their wealth. Money, I also believed, made people mean and greedy. So my subconscious fears kept pushing money away.

I had to learn to deal with my negative feelings about wealth, and then replace them with more positive ones. I had to believe that I could have money *and* be happy, kind and generous. When I was convinced, I was ready to allow prosperity into my life.

At a very early age, we begin attaching our fears and negative beliefs to our image of success. Take the teenager who is doing poorly in school and acting irresponsibly at home. Often, the reason for his behavior is that he's afraid to grow up because he believes that grownups don't have any fun.

My job as a therapist is to help these youngsters see themselves growing up, handling their responsibilities *and* having fun. They have to let go of their fear that being grownup means all work and no play. Once they accomplish this, their behavior usually changes dramatically.

I see success as a delicious red apple that we want very much to eat. But then we imagine there's a worm in it. We're afraid to take even one bite of the apple because we're afraid of the consequences. Creative Therapy teaches us how to remove the worm so we can take

17

a bite of success.

When we're afraid of the possible consequences, we don't take a chance on succeeding. What we must do instead is realistically explore these consequences and then eliminate them.

Recall how frightening consequences prevented me from having a serious relationship after my divorce. I was afraid that being married meant being locked in a cage. Instead, I had to see that it was possible to be married and feel free. Once I had convinced myself of this, the rest was relatively easy.

Although I wasn't even dating anyone at the time, I remember announcing on my 40th birthday in October that I planned to be married by June. Well, I eloped with a wonderful man in April and we held the reception that June.

6. MY PARENTS WON'T LOVE ME IF I'M MORE SUCCESSFUL THAN THEY

You're probably as surprised as I was to hear this one. No client has ever been conscious of this fear, but it continues to come up in the subconscious.

Dennis had been married three times; every time he felt happy in a relationship, he would begin sabotaging it. He would criticize everything his wife did, make mistakes at work and smoke and drink heavily. When he came to me, his third marriage was in trouble.

I learned that Dennis' mother had been very unhappy. And Dennis, being the oldest child, had felt guilty about leaving her to find his own happiness.

She once said to him, "When you leave home and get married, I will no longer be part of your life." Dennis carried that unintentional threat with him into adult life. Without realizing it, he was finding ways to destroy his success and happiness, so that his mother would continue to love him.

Let's face it, times are better for us than they were for our parents, and most of us will end up more successful than they were. Today we all have the potential of living longer than our parents, of making more money, and even of being more successful in our relationships.

Unfortunately, many of us subconsciously believe that it's not right for us to top our parents. And because we feel guilty if we're happier than they, we sabotage our success. Crazy as it sounds, this can happen even if our parents are already deceased.

What we need is permission to be successful and happy. To get that permission, I ask each client to shut his eyes and imagine his parents standing in front of him. Then, he asks his parents if they will continue to love him even if he surpasses their successes.

If the image refuses to grant permission, it doesn't mean lack of love. Rather, it usually means that the parents had their own problems and didn't know how to show their love. So, the next step is visualizing a new set of nurturing parents who will encourage the client to be the best he can be.

7. IF I'M SUCCESSFUL, I WILL BE ACHIEVING MY PARENTS' AMBITIONS, AND I'M ANGRY AT THEM

People who suffer from this last Fear of Success refuse to do well because they don't want to give their parents that satisfaction. Talk about spiting yourself!

Charles' mother dreamed of her son becoming a lawyer or a dentist. But although he did attend law school and later dental school, he couldn't seem to make it. After half-hearted attempts at both professions, he went on to try a string of other jobs. At 50, he had spent most of his adult life at jobs that he hated.

I told Charles to imagine himself as a young boy with his mother standing in front of him.

"What do you want to say to her?" I asked.

"Mom," he said, "I'm furious with you. All you ever did was scream at me or ignore me. You never said anything nice about me. No matter what I did, I couldn't please you. I'll show you. I won't be successful like you want me to be!"

In one session, he pictured himself forgiving his mother. Then he forgave himself for all the years he sabotaged his success. Finally, he decided to succeed for himself.

Do you recognize any of these fears in yourself? If you do, you're certainly not alone. Get in line with the rest of us.

To help you further explore and understand how to conquer your Fear of Success, I've devoted the next nine chapters to clients who came to me for help. They're the stories of everyday people with a common Fear of Success, who were willing to share their very personal experiences in order to help others in similar situations. Each of them is in a different stage of breaking through, as I will let them explain. But I believe they all can eventually reach their goals.

To succeed in your goals, you, like them, have to make the decision that you're tired of being in pain and have suffered enough. You need to say, "I'm ready to do what I need to in order to experience what I want in my life." Then, take one step at a time and go for it!

PART II
The Winners

Chapter 4 _____

Lori's Story:

I'M A BAD PERSON; I DON'T DESERVE TO BE THIN

My problem wasn't unique. I was overweight and couldn't seem to stick to a diet no matter how hard I tried. Every time something in my life went wrong, I would eat. Depression was cause for a binge, and binging made me more depressed so I just ate more.

Ever since I can remember, I dated the wrong guys. With each inevitable breakup, I gained five more pounds. You might say that the story of my life is written on my bathroom scale.

While working with Helene, I found out that eating wasn't my real problem. It was only a symptom. I didn't like myself so I thought I didn't deserve to be thin and attractive. I expressed my pain inside by making myself fat outside.

Even when I lost weight, I still felt fat. For me, fat was a state of mind; it didn't matter how the rest of the world saw me.

When a friend convinced me to go to Helene, I was up to 144 pounds. Even if that's not enormous, I felt like a blimp. I had really hit the bottom of my black hole, a 36-year-old, fat, ugly failure. It seemed like I had failed in everything I'd tried.

I couldn't make it in a marriage; I was unlovable. My husband had divorced me after having an affair with my best friend.

My new boyfriend, Ben, was destroying me, promising to love me if only I would lose weight, if only I wouldn't laugh so loudly, if only I would stop being me. And I was a flop as a mother. Just before my husband walked out, we had adopted a baby girl. She never stopped crying those first few months, probably because that's all she ever saw me do.

I was a very negative, lost person, and felt I deserved what I got. I had a tumor when I was 17, and I never got rid of the feeling that I should have died back then. I didn't know why my life was spared, but I was living on borrowed time, and if felt awful. I couldn't even begin to work with my weight problem; I had too many hurts, too much pain.

It all but destroyed me when I discovered that my husband had been carrying on with my friend, Sheila, who worked with the two of us. I blamed it on myself. I'll never forget the day he walked out on me; I wouldn't let him leave until I'd finished ironing every one of his shirts. Can you believe that? I still felt like the man's servant.

The next day, I filed for divorce, started eating like a pig and began a two-month crying medley. Tom said I was crazy, and he just about convinced me.

In the middle of my desperation, I met Ben, my knight in shining armor. He was a wealthy executive, everything my mother always told me I should want. We lived together off and on—sometimes more off than on—for the next four years. We broke up six major times but I kept going back for more.

Like always, I set myself up to fail in the relationship, this time with someone who didn't want to be tied down to anyone, especially anyone with a kid. Then, when the relationship failed, I could blame myself. I must not be enough; I'm stupid.

I actually believed that I wasn't good enough for Ben. Imagine feeling this way about a man who was stoned out of his mind much of the time on prescription drugs, a man who read my diary without permission and then punished me for a year afterwards. He was reinforcing what I thought of myself, and all the while I thought he was doing me a favor.

El Blimpo! Look at me, I'm a failure. Although it sounds pretty melodramatic now, I had a death wish back then. I tried to drown myself twice in the lake outside our beautiful 4,000-square-foot home. I even failed at that.

In many ways, Ben was just like my mother. When I was a child, she would tell me things like I'd be very pretty if only I'd hold in my stomach. I was her second child, and I don't think she ever wanted me. As far as she could see, I did everything wrong. She was supportive and non-supportive at the same time. She wasn't a holder or a hugger, and I felt like she was always putting me down, constantly laughing at me. She'd say, "I don't know what we're going to do with Lori, she can't do anything right."

Each time she said it, I wanted to die. Instead, I would punish myself, give myself terrible headaches, purposely do things that I knew aggravated my allergies, eat a whole chocolate cake.

Basically, it took four years with Ben to break the umbilical cord to my mother.

After one of our breakups, I went apartment hunting with a friend. I found two places that I could afford: One was a real dump and the other had lots of class. Guess which one I almost rented before my friend brought me to my senses? After all, I was a failure. Among other lessons, my mother had taught me that being a success meant owning a house, and I had already lost two.

By this time, I felt so obese that I was ashamed to go out in public. I used to hide my stomach with my purse so nobody could see my jelly belly.

It was time for help, and I started therapy. Meanwhile, I threw myself into my career. I became a workaholic, while I attempted to prove I was a worthwhile person. In some ways, it paid off because I landed several promotions. Finally, I was beginning to succeed at something, but I couldn't accept it. It didn't fit my image of myself.

So that spring, I ended up in a serious automobile accident, paralyzing the left side of my body. My doctor said I would always walk with a limp, and that I'd never regain full use of my left hand.

I proved him wrong when I typed him a thank you note on my last visit. Although a little weaker than the right, my left hand worked just fine. The truth, I guess, is that being a cripple didn't fit my image of myself either. It's amazing how powerful we all are; we accept what we believe.

When Helene first asked me to close my eyes and visualize myself, I saw a life-size prune, a sad mass of wounds. And even I didn't like shriveled up plums. I realized in that first session that I had a lot of work to do.

I didn't find an instant cure. Although I made some progress, I was still sabotaging myself. Months after I had recuperated from the car accident, I collapsed with mononucleosis. After that, I had a severe asthma attack. The cortisone the doctor gave me for my allergies made me fatter than ever. I was up to 150 pounds, size 16.

But my visualizations were beginning to change. One day I saw myself as a liver that syphons off all the body's impurities. Then I turned into a big ugly tick. The tick reminded me that I was powerful enough to suck out all the old blood to make room for new growth.

In another session, I saw myself climbing a jagged cliff. I was struggling so hard that my hands were raw. It was then that I noticed there was a ladder standing right next to me. I smiled, realizing I didn't have to hurt myself by struggling any longer.

Finally, the picture in my mind turned into a beautiful woman with hair down to her knees. Although she was quite pretty, she was still a little plump. I just couldn't picture myself skinny; I never really thought of myself as slim except, perhaps, when I was ill.

According to Helene, your past makes you what you are today. By letting the pain out and dealing with it, you can let go of your self-hatred. So in the warmth and security of her office, Helene encouraged me to see my mother standing in front of me as she did when I was a child. She was so unforgiving, at least that's how she looked to me. Whatever I did, she criticized me. In one image, I was sick and she was taking care of me. While she acted as martyr, I enjoyed the attention. Maybe that's why I get sick so often.

Through the therapy process, I realized that my mother was really scared herself. She had no friends; I was her whole world and she was jealous of me. She was lonely and insecure. Realizing that has made it possible for me to forgive and love her.

I understand now that I have to do things my way, not the way I think my mother would have liked. I can no longer blame her for my problems; I know she did the best she could.

I wonder why so many of us spend our lives being angry and depiessed when we have the power to be happy? Knowing that I can change myself, make myself into anything I want, gives me a great sense of inner strength and peaceful power.

I have come to believe that I am a valid person who deserves to be happy. Last Christmas, I broke up with Ben for the final time. There's no denying that I still love him, but I certainly no longer like him. I'd rather live without a man than with someone who punishes me for almost everything I do and say.

I feel good about myself. I'm nothing special, but I'm not one of life's losers anymore, either. My daughter is doing fine. We live in a lovely apartment that's packed to the rafters with plants and straw baskets. People tease me about all the clutter, but that's the way I like it.

I'm dating a man I met at a New Year's party. He's warm and supportive, and he genuinely likes doing things with me and my daughter.

He's a big man—6-foot-3, 230 pounds—and he makes me feel petite, although I'm still 20 pounds overweight. I don't know where this relationship will end up, but it doesn't matter. I'm enjoying it, and learning more about myself everyday. If it doesn't work out, I know I won't be destroyed this time. I'm determined not to punish myself any longer. Now that I realize how powerful I am, I don't feel so crushed by other people's behavior.

I must admit that I still have a case of the chubbies. But now when I start binging, I stop to ask myself what's bothering me. For awhile, I was jogging, jumping on my rebounder and lifting weights. But as soon as I started looking good, I stopped. Now, if that's not Fear of Success!

But what if I'm still a little chunky? I've still got a fairly nice body; weight is no longer of prime importance. I feel good and I know when I'm ready, I'll be able to lick the food addiction. When I don't feel the need to punish myself, it seems like I just naturally eat the right foods and the right amount.

I truly believe that I deserve to be successful. That doesn't mean I've eliminated all my fears. When I finally conquer them, I see myself being happily married, making enough money to pamper myself a little, and wearing a size 9.

Still, I hate to let go of those last 20 pounds.

* * * *

I have no doubt that Lori has the power to let go of that weight; she's certainly on her way. All of us perpetuate our symptoms as long as we're getting something out of them. The first and most important step of any so-called diet is to discover the causes of the problem, and Lori has already done that.

We have to ask ourselves: "What do I imagine will happen if I lose weight?" You'll probably be surprised by your answer.

I don't believe that most people are fat simply because they like to eat. Usually, fears are the underlying causes. Fear of Success is present when we want to lose weight, try so hard, and still fail at every attempt. What we need to do is ask ourselves what we're getting out of sabotaging our diet.

There could be many reasons for such behavior. Weight problems, I have found, are caused by each of the seven fears discussed earlier. Many people hide under all seven.

"Being attractive doesn't fit my image of myself," Lori's subconscious told her. "I'm bad, and I don't deserve to be attractive." So weight became a way of mirroring the ugly feeling she had inside. Also, fat was a ready camouflage for her attractiveness. This way, she didn't have to figure out how to handle "undeserved" compliments; she didn't get any.

When they're thin, some women fear that men will be attracted to them only for their bodies. The extra attention would make them feel cheap, so the weight becomes a protection, a cocoon of fat. Women who have been sexually abused often fit into this category.

When one of my clients was a child, she recalls, men would pick her up and toss her into the air. She felt totally powerless. And so she vowed, although subconsciously, that no man would ever be able to mistreat her that way again. And at her current weight of more than 200 pounds, she's right; no man could lift her.

Some women, especially married ones, also gain weight because they don't trust their own passions. They're afraid that if they're attractive, they will be tempted to cheat on their husbands. Since they don't trust themselves, they try to destroy opportunities before they arise. The irony is that while the women believe that the extra girth is saving their marriage, some of their husbands may actually be turned off and look elsewhere.

25

Have you ever noticed that overweight women are usually pretty and even sexy? This is no coincidence. Those who aren't attractive don't need fat for protection.

Some people feel weak and vulnerable when they're thin. "If I'm thin," they believe, "I might get sick and die." Many of these people were sick as children or came from families where there wasn't always enough food to fill their stomachs.

For others, food means love. It's like a fix, it relieves the pain for awhile. When they were young, eating meant getting attention and approval from mom or grandma. So now, they equate slimness with loss of love.

One client told me that although her father had always shown great affection towards her when she was a child, he stopped cuddling her when she turned 13 and started to develop physically. As a teenager, she interpreted this as a sign that he no longer loved her. And since then, she has subconsciously believed that an attractive body means loss of love.

Revenge is another reason why some people stuff themselves. "Mom always told me that if I lost weight, she'd buy me a new wardrobe. Being thin would please my mother, and I'm angry at her. So I'm staying fat."

As you can see, there are many unconscious reasons for being overweight, and Lori was struggling with several of them. When she came to me, I asked her to go back to the time when she decided she was worthless. She saw her mother in front of her, shaking her head disapprovingly and asking, "Lori, what is to become of you?" Lori was just 5 years old. Children look up to their parents as all-knowing, and so she decided she must be bad. Therefore, she believed she deserved criticism. In reality, Lori's decision may have had little or nothing to do with the way her mother really felt.

The best thing parents can do to keep their children from jumping to erroneous decisions like Lori's is to love them unconditionally. Not, "I'll love you if you lose weight," but "I love you because you are you."

We need to learn to separate what they do from who they are. Instead of saying, "Lori, you are fat and bad," we need to say, "Lori, I love you, and I prefer that you eat fruit instead of candy when you are hungry."

We, as parents, have to tell our children that we love them, and hold them in our arms to demonstrate that love. If they feel loved and accepted, they will make the decision that they are important, worthwhile and enough.

Apparently, Lori's mother didn't know how to show that love. And since we all tend to repeat life patterns without even being aware of it, Lori kept attracting people who would treat her like her mother. She found someone to continue the criticism she was used to. If it hadn't been Ben, it would have been someone else just like him.

Not nearly as ironic as it sounds, Ben had his own Fear of Success. He, too, believed he was worthless; so he was the perfect person to help Lori sabotage the relationship. As soon as Lori would get close, he would start pulling away, and vice versa.

In the safety of my office, I encouraged Lori to release the pain of her 5-year-old child. She screamed and cried and beat a pillow. Right there on the mattress, she experienced all the scared, angry and hurt feelings she had blocked for years.

In the past, since it wasn't safe to be angry with her mother, she stifled it with a sarcastic remark or withdrew or stuffed down her anger with food. Overeating, in particular, became her way of getting back at her mother, who always put so much importance on being thin.

It didn't help Lori deal with her feelings about her mother by striking out at Ben; it only perpetuated the problem. She had to learn to deal with her anger in a more constructive way. And she learned that it helped to beat a pillow, scream in the shower and yell at the image of her mother on the wall. Anger is best expressed in private. It doesn't do us any good to lash out at other people, and it isn't fair to them, especially when they aren't the real source of our anger.

The object is to get rid of the intense feelings by ourselves; no one else can—or needs to—handle our incoherent screaming. Then, after we have released the angry energy constructively, we are better able to sit down and discuss the issues calmly and rationally with the person who is triggering our irritation.

After Lori faced her anger, I asked her if she were willing to change that 31-year-old scene, substituting a more nurturing parent. This time, she saw the same little girl holding hands with a mother who told her that she was beautiful and good. Lori heard her say that she loved her very much, that she was glad to be her mother, that she adored her just the way she was. This was a powerful experience for Lori: Her whole body relaxed and she felt peaceful.

Some people protest that by altering the original experience, we're falsifying the truth. But I believe that we're actually "truthifying" the past. The truth is that every human being is basically good, important, worthwhile and lovable. The truth is that Lori is okay; it was her mother who didn't feel okay. The process of visualization merely helped Lori get in touch with these truths.

Based on her new experience, Lori was able to start re-owning and loving the part of herself that I refer to as the "scared kid." No matter how old we are, we all have a scared little boy or girl inside of us. That's the part that believes all our negative decisions. By taking care of that part, Lori was able to make a new decision: She was a worthwhile person.

Realistically, she can't expect to change her old opinions of herself overnight; it takes time and energy. So, Lori had to continue to visualize her nurturing mother and make affirmations to herself. She wrote her affirmations on a card, which she kept in her wallet, and repeated them daily. "I, Lori, am a worthwhile person." Soon, she began to believe the new, positive decision.

We all have a tape recorder inside our heads. Lori's old tape, the one she had replayed all her life, said she was worthless. Now, she has a new tape, which she has to keep reinforcing until it becomes stronger and louder, drowning out the old, negative one.

Lori no longer needs to be fat to punish herself, because she no longer sees herself as a worthless 5-year-old. Odd as it seems, our image of ourselves often has nothing to do with the way we really look. Lori has always been a very attractive, warm and loving person. Even when I met her last year as a frightened, confused woman, I immediately liked her. My job was to help her see and appreciate what I and other people saw in her.

Lori has one final Fear of Success to conquer—fear of the unknown—before she can give up those last 20 pounds and accept herself as an attractive person. "What will it be like to be a perfect size 9?"

Like the bearded man who's afraid to shave off his whiskers, most of us are somewhat afraid of the unfamiliar. But now, at least, Lori has the tools to deal with the unknown.

Chapter 5

Mark's Story:

RELATIONSHIPS MEAN RESPONSIBILITY AND PAIN

Meeting new people and starting new relationships was relatively easy for me. The hard part was taking a chance on sticking with them, nurturing them, and allowing them to grow.

You don't have to be particularly attractive or super sophisticated to play musical beds. At least, I didn't have much trouble, and I'm certainly no hunk. For a long time, sex was the most important part of my relationships, although it's difficult to explain why. I guess sex was a substitute for lots of other things: A chance to be close without really getting close. An easy investment, because it didn't cost me much emotionally.

Moving out of the bedroom into something more permanent scared the hell out of me. I couldn't handle the tremendous responsibility. On the other hand, I was petrified that if I did commit myself, the woman would turn around and dump me anyway.

So I moved from one singles bar to another; from one disastrous affair to the next. It was safe but unbearably lonely. Because I wasn't sure I could hold onto any one person, I ran around with a whole bunch. And because I ran around, my fear became reality: I couldn't hold on to one person.

When I started working with Helene, I was depressed and lonely. I was getting nowhere fast. I wanted a special woman in my life, and I was doing everything I could to sabotage that goal. My wife died in 1976, leaving me with two young girls. And my last girlfriend had left me to marry another man. I couldn't seem to concentrate on anything, especially my work as a mechanical engineer.

I had married right after my hitch in Vietnam—to a pen pal from New Zealand. Although we had been corresponding for about a year, we'd actually spent only one week together. We had two children right away, but the marriage was a disaster from the beginning.

I hadn't dated much, and I resented having my freedom taken away from me by this woman who was practically a stranger. I didn't know how to talk to her, and she resented the fact that I didn't try. She criticized me constantly, blamed me for everything that went wrong. No matter what I did, it wasn't enough to make her happy. Once, she went so far as to accuse me of molesting our oldest daughter. That really hurt me.

Three months after our youngest was born, we discovered that my wife, Marlena, had breast cancer, which had already spread throughout her body. As her pain increased, our relationship continued to deteriorate.

If she hadn't been so ill, I'm sure we would have been divorced. Meantime, I resented the responsibility of taking care of her, and I resented her for putting me through it. Sometimes, God forgive me, I actually wished she were dead. Two years after the cancer was discovered, Marlena died, leaving me alone with the girls. I felt relief, anger, fear and most of all, guilt.

The tension during her illness had been impossible, and I started looking for companionship almost immediately after she died. First, I met someone at my daughter's day care center, and from her, I moved on to a succession of women. I felt safe having a different one every week, and I didn't have trouble finding them. I think the fact that I was a widower helped, because they all felt sorry for me.

I wasn't picky about whom I slept with, but I never gave much of myself. I was resigned to being single at least until the girls grew up. Maybe it was a lack of self-esteem or simply the fear of a permanent commitment, but I didn't expect to find anyone who was interested in marrying me. I was scared that if I let myself get involved with someone, she would end up walking out on me. After all, in a very real sense, my wife had deserted me.

I was so scared of being dumped that I always made sure I walked out first. Whenever I felt threatened, I would get angry and withdraw. I wasn't one to confront the problem; instead, I would hold in my anger and build up reasons for taking off.

Through therapy, I realized that I had developed my pattern of running away from my father. Everytime he got bored or something went wrong at work, he would pack up and move the entire family with him to a new city. By the time I finished high school, I had gone to 13 different schools, sometimes two in one term. I was always the new kid on the block, and as soon as I made friends, we'd end up moving on.

While my father was following his rainbow, he left the care of the four kids up to my mother. Burdened with so much responsibility, she tried to pawn much of it off on me. But I did a lot of resisting, especially of the seemingly endless chores.

I continued my childhood pattern into adult life. To me, relationships have always meant responsibility, and so I resisted them. Otherwise, ironically, I have a tendency to bear the responsibility of everything, even when it's not mine. Although I resent it, I feel compelled to take care of people, because that's how I was brought up to behave.

When I met my girlfriend Bonnie three years ago, I think I tried too hard to take care of her. We met at a seminar, and began a long-distance affair. But whenever we got together, we drove each other crazy.

I couldn't keep up with her moods. One minute she was extremely warm, the next, as cold as ice. All the time we were supposed to be seeing each other exclusively, we were cheating. Once, she told me that I would be better off finding someone nice and loving. I told her that I didn't want someone nice, that I wanted her.

If I'd been smart, I would have bailed out then. As it was, I put a lot of effort into that relationship; writing, telephoning and commuting back and forth. Then, one day out of the clear blue, she told me that she'd met someone else and was planning to marry him.

I felt relieved and devastated, not to mention angry. Most of that anger was at myself because I hadn't been the one to call it quits.

I decided then that I'd never let another woman hurt me. So it wasn't surprising that my next fling didn't last long. After I had been dating the woman less than a month, we got into a fight about sex. I walked out and never saw her again. The problem, obviously, wasn't really sex; I just used it as an excuse.

I met my present wife, Ann, at one of Helene's Fear of Success seminars, and we ended up in the same counseling group. Ann was different from most of the others I'd dated; she could take care of herself. She even had her own cabin cruiser. We started dating regularly, and before long, we were getting pretty close. I predicted very early in the relationship that I would marry her.

Then, I spent the next five months retreating from that position. The closer we got, the more I ran around with other women. I even bragged to Ann about my exploits, and we ended up fighting about anything and everything.

Fortunately, my therapy group helped me understand why we were having so many meaningless arguments. Often, when couples are afraid to say what they want and need, they pick a fight with each other. Instead of telling Ann that I needed some space, I would start an argument about something completely different.

Helene pointed out that couples don't have to hurt each other to make time for themselves. How much easier simply to say, "I love you and I need space." That way you get time alone without making the other person think that she did something wrong.

I've really got to give Ann a lot of credit; no matter what I did to sabotage the relationship, she hung in there. Everytime I panicked and walked out, she'd wait patiently for me to come back. It became apparent that I would have to do something awfully bad to make her bail out.

Although I don't remember most of my dreams, I do remember one particular one during that period. I dreamed that my dead wife was still alive haunting me. She wouldn't let go, and I knew I would be forced to take care of her forever. I yelled and screamed at her, told her that I had been to her funeral, that I even had her death certificate to prove she was dead. It wasn't my fault she died, I told her, and I wasn't going to continue punishing myself forever. That night, she finally disappeared from my life, along with a big part of my guilt about her death.

Ann and I eventually moved in together and started discussing marriage. With four kids between us, we talked about the practicality of buying a van. The night we were to finalize the deal, I really panicked. Buying a van together certainly wasn't as scary as a commitment of marriage, but at $12,000, it was a medium-sized commitment. I started packing. Then, all of a sudden, I stopped; the fear had subsided.

We were married soon after that. I can't say I had completely changed. I kept an old, separate checking account as my security blanket. At times, I missed my freedom and was on the verge of leaving. But the feeling always passed before I did anything drastic. I learned that fear didn't have to run my life. I guess if everyone took off everytime they got scared, there wouldn't be any relationships.

One night, I had another dream: I was having an affair with a woman at work and she was furious when I told her I was married. She demanded that I leave my wife. But I told her, "No way." I think that was a real turning point for Ann and me. In my subconscious, I had finally made the permanent commitment I'd always feared. I was tired of running.

Feeling self-satisfied the next morning, I decided to splurge on an expensive electric train set I'd been wanting for a long time. I was beginning to re-own the happy-kid part of me, and allowing myself the time to play. I deserve to have some fun in my life; everyone does.

But the heavy burden of responsibility still gets to me sometimes. The funny thing is that it isn't directed at anything in particular. Even the extra two kids don't really scare me, although I'm not quite sure what my role should be with them.

I never did hear the proverbial bells for Ann; my heart didn't race or my legs get weak. Our relationship is based on warmth and friendship, and I think that's more than enough to sustain it. Ann gets a little irritated when I say it's a comfortable marriage, but I mean that in the most positive sense. We enjoy each other's company, we can talk to each other and laugh together. I guess you could say that our one-year marriage is already as comfortable as an old pair of shoes. And what's wrong with that? There's nothing so dependable.

I still miss my freedom once in awhile but I no longer panic. I'm comfortable and I don't feel the need to move. Why go out to look for hamburger when you have steak on the table?

In fact, I think I'll spring for steak tonight. I still have $22.00 in my own checking account, and it's time that I closed it out.

*   *   *   *

"Come close," Mark told the women in his life, "but stay away."

"Come close," most of us say. "I want to love you, share with you, play with you, build a life and family together. But stay away. If I get too close, you will see how ugly I am. If we get too intimate, you will see that I'm not enough, that I'm a bad person. I'm afraid that I won't be able to please you, that you will take away my freedom and hurt me. I'm afraid that I'll have to give up myself in order to satisfy you." We drive each other crazy with these mixed messages.

Mark, for one, has certainly come a long way by allowing himself to love Ann. Notice, however, he never mentions the word love, although he obviously loves his wife and has a beautiful, healthy relationship with her.

He hasn't quite crossed all his barriers yet; a part of him is still holding back. Because he doesn't completely believe that he deserves happiness, he allows himself to be just a little happy.

When Mark came to me, he confessed that he was afraid of getting hurt. Hurt is one of the scariest consequences we connect with our image of success. We're afraid that if we take a chance, we'll get hurt. So to protect ourselves, we push people away and sabotage our relationships.

When clients tell me they really want a special person in their life but all they're experiencing is rejection, I suggest that they close their eyes and visualize their heart. Often, they see it encased in iron, bruised or stabbed with arrows or swords. They vividly see that they're still nursing wounds from past relationships.

Such people commonly build tall, thick walls around themselves. The walls keep them safe, but lonely.

So we work on releasing their past pains and increasing their self-esteem. When they feel good about themselves, they're not devastated when someone doesn't want to be with them. Instead, they move on to meet people who will appreciate them.

When their hearts look healed and healthy, they're ready to carve out a door in their walls. They're ready to step outside and allow others to get close to them. Almost miraculously, as soon as they overcome the fear of getting hurt, their relationships begin to flourish.

Underneath Mark's fear of getting hurt was a fear that he wasn't enough, a decision he made as a young boy. Since he was constantly moving from home to home, he always felt like an outsider. As soon as he made any friends, he had to leave them. Mark learned that when you get close to people, you have to leave them. That hurt too much, so he resolved in his subconscious that he wouldn't get close to anyone.

Fear of a successful relationship is one of our most common fears. It's no wonder that so many marriages end in divorce.

Many of us grew up watching and feeling the pain in our parents' relationships. Although unhappy, the majority chose to stick it out ostensibly "for the children."

As a result, we as children often felt guilty. We also decided that marriage means pain. So what do we do? We end up marrying partners that fit our belief system, and we end up in pain, too.

Divorce is often the only workable alternative to an unsalvageable marriage. And, although it has a bad reputation, divorce in itself is not necessarily bad. We live longer today than past generations, and we have more choices. Getting the most out of life has become far more important than mere survival.

The prosperity of the last 20 years has shaken us. Many people who've made a lot of money and are outwardly successful are realizing that they're miserable inside. And so they're beginning to evaluate their lives, including their relationships. They're beginning to take control of their lives, rather than let society run them.

Today, many people are seeking something more important than a mere marriage certificate. Their primary goal has become inner peace and happiness. They're discovering that if they're not happy, they have the power, courage, support and opportunity to move on.

Mark stayed in an unhappy first marriage out of an overbearing sense of duty and guilt. His fear of this kind of responsibility kept him for a long time from committing himself to another woman.

As a boy, he learned from his mother that life is a struggle, and that women make you take care of them. We all have a tendency to marry our mothers or fathers, especially if we're still angry, hurt or resentful towards them. If, for example, our parents made us feel like caretakers, as Mark's mother did, we find a woman who needs to be taken care of.

Mark did just that. His first wife was weak and demanding. On top of that, she ended up terminally ill, demanding even more attention. Finally she died, leaving Mark with the responsibility of two children. Just like his mother had taught him, life was indeed a struggle. No wonder responsibility petrified him!

To Mark, a relationship meant responsibility, and responsibility meant having no time for himself. One day in therapy, I asked him to close his eyes and visualize the word "responsibility" written in the clouds. The letters filled the sky, terrifying him.

I asked him to finish the statement, "Responsibility means to me. . . ." His response: "Responsibility means no time for myself, no time to play."

I guided him back to the time when he first decided that. He was a boy and his mother was saying things that made him feel guilty for not sharing some of her responsibilities. He had decided then that since grownups have no fun, he didn't want to grow up.

I hear this same fear repeatedly from my teenage clients: "Why should I grow up? Grownups don't have any fun. All they do is work, pay bills and worry. If I grow up, I can't have any fun."

Do you hear the Fear of Success? Many young people make the equation, "If I grow up, then I won't have any fun."

When I ask them if they would be willing to grow up if they could still enjoy themselves, they almost always answer yes. So I help them see themselves as adults having fun—and feeling good.

To me, growing up means accepting certain responsibilities, especially the responsibility for yourself and your own happiness. But that still leaves plenty of time for having fun. A healthy person is one who can balance work and play.

Remember Mark's trains? As a child, he never played. Now, at last, he has given himself permission to enjoy himself. He's taking time to do some of the playing he missed when he was young.

But before Mark could allow himself to play, he had to change the negative decisions that were holding him back. The first step was releasing the anger he felt towards his parents and first wife for dumping so much responsibility on him. When I encouraged him to release that anger in my office, he was like a bomb, attacking and ripping apart the pillows.

After his anger subsided, I asked him if he was willing to change his childhood image of his mother. He was. And in a new visualization, he saw his mother taking care of herself, while she encouraged him to go outside and play with his friends. He saw his mother appreciate the things he did for her and thank him for being such a good son.

From the new scene, he was able to come to some positive realizations: He realized that he had helped his mother, that he was a good son. He also realized that there are many women in the world who can take care of themselves. He made the affirmation, "I Mark, am in a fulfilling relationship and I am sharing the responsibilities with my partner."

Next, Mark had to deal with his guilt concerning his first wife's death. It's classic to feel responsible for someone else's death and to punish yourself. In one counseling session, I asked Mark to imagine that he was a judge, accusing himself of causing his wife's death. He did, and he saw that he had sentenced himself to five years of misery. He still had three months to go, and he actually waited them out before he allowed himself to commit to Ann—a wonderful, loving woman.

By changing his old image of a wife, which was modeled by his mother, he was able to find a spouse who was both loving and independent. And by getting rid of the subconscious tapes that equated a relationship with pain, responsibility and guilt, Mark discovered that a loving relationship can mean sharing, joy, fun, and excitement.

Chapter 6 _____

Janet's Story:

NO MAN WANTS A SUCCESSFUL CAREER WOMAN

I was convinced that I had the prescription for the ideal life. I was finally "Mrs. Dr.," an M.R.S. basking in my husband's M.D.

So I certainly wasn't prepared when it hit me, like an unexpected flu bug in the middle of summer: Dr. Steven Lloyd wanted a divorce.

Well, he got his freedom, along with the motorcycle and the Mercedes; I got the house, the station wagon, the three kids and my hangups about earning a living.

Brought up in the Midwest in the 1950s, I held the same beliefs as the rest of the women of my generation: The man supports his family financially, while the woman supports him emotionally. The perfect wife is supportive, dependent and passive. No man wants an independent woman, especially if she makes a good living on her own.

My mother never worked; in fact, she didn't know how to drive a car or even balance a checkbook. I learned from her that men are intimidated by successful women, and I just accepted the fact that I couldn't have both a career and a marriage.

Sure, I went to college. That's where middle-class girls went to find a husband, and to get a teaching credential just in case anything ever happened to that husband. With those goals accomplished, I signed on temporarily as a kindergarten teacher so that I could put my young husband through medical school.

As soon as he completed his residency, I quit my job. All I ever wanted to be was a wife and mother. We moved to California, where Steve set up practice and I became the "doctor's wife." Everything was going as prescribed. I had a near-perfect life; my biggest problem was what to cook for dinner.

Then one day I woke up to find myself the ex-Mrs. Dr. I was

panic-stricken. Although I still believed I needed a man to take care of me, I no longer thought I was worthy of a man.

It was 12 years ago that I sold our house, piled the children into the station wagon and moved to a new town to do heaven knows what. Since I couldn't find a job as a teacher, I settled for one as a teacher's aide. For $3.72 an hour I worked in one of those "open classrooms" where the students sit on pillows and learn to spell only "when they're ready."

Between the pittance I earned and the child support that Steve kicked in, we managed to get by. But I felt overwhelmed. I was chief cook and bottle washer, nursemaid, mother and father; I was playing so many roles that I didn't have time to be me.

One day a friend offered me a job as his assistant in the commercial real estate business. Perfect. I was comfortable in the role of man's assistant.

So for the next few years I typed, served coffee, and learned the tricks of selling and leasing property. Meanwhile my social life settled into a comfortable routine. I was dating a man who, like my father and husband, believed that there was only one captain of the ship—and he was it. I certainly never told him otherwise. I was too scared to rock the boat!

I was 45 years old, struggling to get by on a measly $12,000 salary, and wondering which way to turn, when I met Helene. I needed someone to help me decide what to do with my life.

It's funny how you can be headed straight for disaster and feel safe at the same time. Even though my life was crummy, I was secure in my pain.

I've since discovered that life is like freefalling from an airplane. You can either stay in your seat and watch the world whiz by or you can take the plunge. Although it looks so scary from the door, the hardest part is letting go. Once you do it's exhilarating. The fall isn't so bad, and it gives you the confidence to try again and again.

To prepare for my jump, I first had to release all the anger I had bottled up inside me. I started with my parents. I hated my insensitive, domineering father who was in large part responsible for my fear and resentment towards men. My God, he used to drag me into the bathroom, pull down my panties and beat me with his belt. Then he'd lock me in our dark basement for hours. No matter how hard I tried to be a good girl, he would find an excuse to beat me.

And my mother, that miserably unhappy women, did nothing to stop him. I guess she was afraid of him, too. As her own frustrations mounted, she just sat back and blamed everyone else, including me. She didn't believe she had any options and she passed that belief on to her children. Her legacy to me was a bag full of "shoulds" and "oughts" that I never managed to live up to.

But at last I was beginning to understand her; dealing with my father took more time. In one counseling session, I imagined that he was sitting on a pillow and I killed him with a rubber knife. Then I imagined I blew up our horrible basement. Those things accomplished, I replaced my father with a loving parent.

During another session, I piled up a pyramid of pillows, each one representing the men in my life. Then I defiantly jumped up and down on them, crushed them, and left them strewn around the room. I, Janet Lloyd, wanted to be on top for a change. I was tired of letting other people stomp on me.

I worked often with visualizations, seeing myself as I wanted to be. Then I actually drew a picture of myself sitting behind a big, impressive desk. The caption said, "I am capable; I have the job I want; I have all the money I want; I am successful; my work is satisfying in all respects. I have a wonderful man in my life."

I was on my way, and in time, I really started to believe that it was possible for me to have a complete life, including both a man and a good career.

In fact, I actually created my current job as a commercial real estate broker when I decided that it was what I wanted. I simply walked into the office of one of the big real estate companies in town and presented my proposal.

I continued using the visualization process in my work. I pictured one of my clients moving into an 11,000-square-foot bookstore. I even drew a picture of the building with the name across the top. Four months later, he moved into that very building, and I earned a $40,000 commission!

I drew a picture of another client in a new Chinese restaurant, and a third in a computer store. Both eventually moved into buildings that looked surprisingly similar to my sketches.

The only time the visualizations didn't work was when I really didn't believe them. As soon as I began to doubt myself, I ran into trouble. I was about to close one deal, for example, when I started thinking that I hadn't really earned the $16,000 commission. The next morning, the deal fell through.

On the whole, however, I was beginning to believe in myself, and my career was taking off. In just a few years, I was making $75,000 a year. And that was during a recession.

In the past, I had always seen myself as a victim of circumstance. But now I understand that nobody has to be a victim, that people victimize themselves. Everyone is responsible for his or her own life; we have the power to be whatever we want to be.

Unfortunately, I over-compensated for past mistakes. To make up for my femininity, which I considered a hindrance in the business world, I set out to prove that I was better than any man.

39

I dumped the "captain" I had been dating for four years and moved on to other conquests. I reversed the male-female role as I saw it, and began treating men as sex objects. The game was to see how many men I could lure into my bed.

One day it dawned on me that all the men I was seeing were married. I guess I felt safer that way. At that point, I decided to end my campaign. Although I went home from one singles' party without an escort, I wasn't empty-handed. I had earned an $800 commission by leasing one of my buildings.

Last year was the best year of my life. My job went great, I redecorated our home, and I was able to send my youngest daughter on a one month vacation in Europe. I even made peace with my mother who has been living with us since my father died.

I've been doing quite a bit of soul searching lately and I've discovered that the universe is really a very generous place. It gives good things to each of us as long as we're ready to receive.

I, for one, am getting ready to accept what I want. I've already let go of a great deal of pain and fear. But it's no miracle. I think too many people expect success to land in their laps; they're not willing to work for it. I believe that we have to make all our own miracles.

So far I've been working on feeling good about myself. Now I'm getting ready to add a fulfilling relationship to my life. I'm convinced there are many men in this world who aren't intimidated by a successful career woman. I'd be an excellent "catch" for any one of them. I'm a good person and I deserve a good man.

Since I've begun to realize that I deserve the best, it's much easier to decide what I truly want out of life. This time I want an equal relationship; I no longer need a man to prop me up. I want a man who will accept me just the way I am, lock, stock and idiosyncrasies.

I'm just going to put out to the universe that I'm ready for a real soul connection. I've already started to visualize him. He will be my best friend, honest, sincere, sophisticated and prosperous.

At this point in my life I feel sorry for women who have settled for less than they deserve. Many of them are bored with being "Mrs. Mr.," but they don't know any other way. They never took the opportunity to develop and now they're too scared. They've become comfortable in their silk cocoons.

I'm glad that I was kicked out of mine and forced to survive in the world. I'm happy I'm me; I've done a hell of a job at work and at home.

Now, I want a man who is as prosperous as I. The way I figure it, I may as well continue to live in style.

Like the child who crawls before she learns to walk, we need to take our growth step by step. Janet started with her career and it's no surprise that she succeeded. She already had the intelligence and training; all she needed was the desire and determination to break through her Fear of Success, the fear that no man wants a successful career woman.

I don't believe in coincidence or luck. We just have to get out of our own way, stop blocking ourselves, and allow things to happen. Look at the handicapped people who learn to do incredible feats. The only thing that limits us is ourselves, our own belief systems. Janet didn't have to do anything physically different in order to earn that first $40,000 commission. She just had to change some of her beliefs and feel different inside.

Before Janet could believe that she deserved and could have both a career and a man, she needed to discover her true self. After years of leaving her fate up to the men in her life, she had to reclaim her own power and learn to use and enjoy it. She had to experience her independence and feel that she was a worthwhile person. I have found that people who believe they don't deserve good things often say they don't know what they want. But as soon as they decide that they are worthy of happiness, their pathway becomes clear.

People who enter relationships before they themselves feel whole do so for the wrong reasons. When Janet is ready to make room in her life for a special man, it will be because she *wants* him, not because she *needs* him. At the rate she has been growing, I don't think that time is far off.

Knowing Janet today, it's difficult to envision the frightened, anxious and confused woman that came to me for help. Feeling helpless is paralyzing, yet she was afraid to feel powerful. Hers was a classic case of being afraid to stay where she was and afraid to move on. That's what I call being stuck.

Janet came to me as an actress, replaying the old negative roles in a real-life drama, where there were only victims, persecutors and rescuers. Her father was a persecutor and her husband was a rescuer, before he, too, turned into a persecutor.

All the while, Janet played the lead as the helpless victim, standing in for her mother. Ironically, although Janet had little respect for her mom, she followed her life script without question.

That's not as unusual as it sounds; for regardless of what we think of our parents, we tend to model ourselves after them. Unconsciously we believe, "I'm a woman like my mother so I must act the same way."

Our society is responsible for casting us in these roles, with men having to rescue women. And since we resent the parts we're forced to play, we often blame each other. Relationships and families are destroyed, and we all end up as losers.

Janet's entire family was losing, even her father. He was a troubled man who took out his frustrations on his daughter. The beatings, I believe, were a manifestation of his sexual problems.

It's normal for fathers to have sexual feelings towards their daughters but it's certainly not okay in our society to *act* on them. Usually these feelings emerge when the daughter is about five and again when she reaches puberty.

Some men are so frightened by these feelings that they either push away their daughters or, worse, beat them. The young girls make a decision that they're not lovable, when the truth is they're too lovable.

What fathers need to do is accept the normalcy of such feelings, and give themselves permission to feel this way without guilt. If they don't, chances are they will be angry with themselves and, unfortunately, project that anger onto their daughters.

Janet's father was a very angry man. His daughter interpreted his anger and the subsequent beatings as proof that she was a bad person. And, because she wasn't worthwhile, she believed that she didn't deserve to be happy with either a career or a man. Besides, she believed that no man would want a financially successful wife.

Janet's Fear of Success led her to date married men; that way, she didn't have to worry about a permanent involvement. Her one night stands reflected her anger towards her father and men in general. She felt powerful enticing men into her bed and leaving them in the morning.

How many men do you know who treat women this way? Generally, it's an act of anger and fear: "I'll give you my body, but not myself." Promiscuity makes them feel less vulnerable.

Although this type of revenge isn't necessarily a "male" trait, it can be part of the macho training. And Janet, who had been taught that femininity and high achievement are mutually exclusive, was in training. When she finally did stop blocking the masculine side of her nature, she overdid it.

Often, in the growth process, we need to go to extremes before we can get back to center. From there, we can go in either direction when appropriate. A balanced individual is able to combine the so-called masculine "thinking" traits, like logic, power, strength and assertiveness, with the more feminine "feeling" ones like gentleness, lovingness, creativity and vulnerability.

Actually, there have always been successful career women who manage to have happy personal relationships, too. Women's Liberation simply put the stamp of approval on them. And as more women begin to free themselves from their roles as victims, men will be freed from their roles as rescuers. Women's liberation has opened the door to men's liberation.

It's true that women may "lose" a man or two by not playing the game, by competing in the business world, but men's egos are not women's problem. If we feel rejected by a man because he can't accept our equality, then he isn't the right one for us in the first place.

And after re-owning her power, Janet for one is certainly ready to be an equal partner. Real power is self-confidence: Janet is successful because she feels powerful inside. As a result of that feeling, she has achieved financial success. That success, in turn, has reinforced her belief in herself. Janet is in a very powerful cycle because success leads to success.

There are many men today who are looking for successful career women; they're tired of carrying the financial burden alone. If you haven't been able to meet such a man yourself, perhaps it's because you really don't believe you can. Your fears may have become self-fulfilling prophesies.

Now that Janet believes she's entitled to both a career and a fulfilling relationship, she's ready to allow that special man into her life.

Chapter 7

Ellen's Story:

A RELATIONSHIP MEANS SEXUAL DEMANDS

Sex has always reminded me of vegetables. No matter how distasteful, they're necessary evils. You eat vegetables to make you strong and healthy; you tolerate sex to get and keep a man.

Sure, I have sexual relations with the men in my life. Nowadays, it's difficult to have even a casual date without ending up in bed together. Men expect it.

The problem is that even though I agree to play by the rules, my relationships never last more than a couple of months. I've developed a pattern: I meet an attractive man, we go out, and we end up in bed together. Not long after that, I get bored and start looking around for someone else.

The strange part is that despite my poor track record, I want a loving relationship more than anything else in the world. This singles' scene has become a royal pain. I'm a 47-year-old divorcee with five grown children. It's about time I settled down. There must be some way to combine love and sex in a fulfilling, lasting relationship.

Ever since I was a child the thought of sex has left me cold. I can remember many a night lying in bed, listening to my parents fight about it. My dad never seemed to get enough and my mother didn't want any part of it. I don't think she ever had any sexual feelings.

But when Dad was in the mood, Mother didn't have a choice. She either gave in or got hurt. One night I remember I heard her screaming. It sounded worse than usual so I decided to check things out. What I found when I opened my parents' door was horrifying. My mother was lying on the floor between the twin beds crying; her left eye was bruised and her nose was bleeding. How ugly and painful sex seemed to me at that moment!

My parents kicked me out of the room and neither of them ever mentioned the incident to me again. In fact, sex was never discussed in our house. All I knew was that it resulted in lots of children—my mother had 10 of them—and that meant a heavy responsibility. I should know; I was the one stuck with helping look after my younger sisters and brothers.

Since I couldn't see anything good about it, I was content to ignore sex until I was forced to deal with it. The time came when I was married at 19 years old. I think my wedding night was one of the worst experiences of my life. It had been a long, tiring day of partying. All I really wanted to do was lie in Jeff's arms and rest. I was terrified of making love. But I didn't know how to explain my feelings to Jeff, and so I decided to lie still and let him do whatever he wanted to me.

I was cold and unresponsive and intercourse turned out to be as bad as I had imagined. Since Jeff hadn't had any previous experience either, he was rough and insensitive. He didn't know anything about foreplay; he just rammed his penis into my vagina. It hurt even more than I had expected. I felt like I was being raped and there was nothing I could do about it. After all, Jeff was my husband with every right to demand my body.

It might have helped if I'd had a close friend or confidante, but there was no one I felt I could trust; least of all a gynecologist. Soon after I was married, I developed a vaginal infection. I found a gynecologist in the telephone book, and since I'd never been to one before, I didn't know what to expect.

Alone with me in his office, he told me to put my feet up in the metal stirrups. Then he bent over me and started listening to my heart with his stethoscope. Before I realized what was happening, he started massaging my vagina. He said that he had to do this in order to check out my heartrate. And me in my naivete just lay there and let him carry on.

He got me so aroused that I felt lightheaded. The feeling scared me and I think I blacked out for a few moments. When he had finished, I still wasn't sure what had actually happened. All I knew was that I felt dirty. In a panic I ran out of that so-called "doctor's" office and home to my husband.

But I never told Jeff what had happened. I just pushed it out of my mind. Meantime our own sexual relationship seemed to improve a little; at least we had plenty of sex. Jeff tried to be more patient, experimenting with ways to make me happy. I actually started warming up to him although I never did allow myself to get excited and turned on.

Neither of us had heard of an orgasm for women. I hit upon my first one by accident ten years after we were married. One night I was lying in bed with Jeff, listening to the stereo. Without thinking, I began stimulating myself in time to the music. When I worked myself up to an orgasm, I was as surprised as Jeff.

We have five children together, although we planned only four. Something went wrong with my diaphragm. Actually I thought we were a reasonably happy family right up until the time Jeff hit me with divorce papers. He told me that the only thing he needed from me was sex and he complained that our sex life was lousy. He accused me of being aloof and disinterested. I didn't argue with him; he was probably right. And I felt like a complete failure, because marriage was supposed to be forever.

To figure out what to do next, I went to a psychologist recommended by a friend. Believe it or not, I ended up having intercourse with him right on his office rug. I don't know why I let it happen. I was feeling very vulnerable and he took advantage of that vulnerability—the jerk. He told me that he could teach me how to enjoy sex and I believed in him. Besides, I'd been taught that you do what men say. I knew that he didn't love me and sex with him was no better or worse than it had been before. I didn't expect much and I didn't get much. We had sex six times before I mustered the courage to tell him to go to hell.

After that experience, I decided it was time I learned something about this mysterious thing called sex. I read dozens of books that I should have read long before and I did some experimenting. Since then I've been to bed with a succession of men; not that I consider myself promiscuous. I usually end up dating—and sleeping with—one or two men a year. But an unfulfilling sexual experience always seems to stand between me and a lasting relationship.

To figure out why I wasn't attracting the kind of man I thought I wanted, I started therapy with Helene six months ago. In one of my first guided imageries, I went back to the time that I'd seen my father abuse my mother. After I had relived it and expressed my anger and repulsion, I changed that scene in my mind. This time when I opened my parents' bedroom door, I saw my mother and father cuddling and acting very lovingly towards each other.

Looking back on the situation, I feel sorry for my parents. I imagine my mother was afraid to become pregnant again and didn't know how to tell my father. Because he didn't understand, my dad probably felt hurt and neglected.

My old tapes hadn't explained any of this to me. All I knew as a child was that sex made my mother unhappy, and I modeled my frigidity after hers. It's scary how easy it is to perpetuate feelings like this. I'm afraid I've allowed the same thing to happen to my own son. At 19 years old, he has been unable to ejaculate with his girlfriend. I wonder if this isn't his way of holding back like me and his grandmother.

Fortunately, with therapy and more visualizations, I'm beginning to overcome some of my hangups. After dealing with my parents, I moved on to my husband, replaying in a visualization the trauma of my wedding night. This time I was so angry at Jeff for not understanding my feelings that I kicked him out of bed. That accomplished, I changed the scene to one in which my husband was content to hold me, cuddle me, and assure me of his love. I felt all warm and loving.

From my new perspective, I see that neither Jeff nor I was prepared for a sexual relationship. Jeff didn't mean to hurt me; he just didn't know any better. If I had been able to communicate my feelings to him—tell him that I was tired and scared—perhaps things might have turned out differently for us. In my imagination, I apologized to Jeff for putting all the blame on him.

I think I was angrier at my gynecologist than anyone else. In one of my most terrifying visualizations, I found myself back on his examining table with my feet up. You know the position. This time, though, I wasn't about to lie still for the humiliation. I beat him off me with my legs; I kicked and kicked and kicked. Then I pictured myself in court with him as the defendant and me as judge. I convicted him of sexual assault, labeled him a sick man, and committed him to a mental hospital. Then I imagined myself returning to his empty office. This time I was in control.

I went through a similar exercise with the psychologist, seeing myself with the power to ward off his advances.

In just a few months with Helene, I was beginning to see and understand why sex had always been so distasteful to me. Because I believed that men wanted women only for their bodies, I created men in my life who wanted just that. I now see that marrying Jeff and ending up in sexual situations with my doctors, as well as the rest of the men in my life, was no coincidence. It was a self-fulfilling prophesy. "See," I could say to myself, "you were right. Men use women for their sexual pleasure."

When I began to believe that this wasn't true, I could start attracting a more loving, affectionate kind of man. And I did. A few weeks after I started visualizing such a man, I met Matt at a dance.

I was determined not to let myself get in the way of this relationship and I made up my mind to leave all my old prejudices behind. I simply wanted to let things happen.

Yes, we did end up in bed. But this time it was because I wanted to, not because I felt obligated. Matt was different from all the other men I had dated; he never pushed me. He was an exceptionally affectionate man who was content to spend hours just cuddling. He reminded me of a teddy bear. Sex with him was wonderful; he was so warm and caring. As for me, I was anything but frigid. For the first time I experienced an orgasm during intercourse, a bonus I'd never even hoped for. That relationship proved to me that sex could be sensual and very enjoyable.

Matt and I broke up after a few months. It turned out that Matt, who had just been through a divorce, had some issues to solve by himself. So we said goodbye without blame or excuses, and we went our separate ways to continue our own growth. I had learned what I needed to learn with him and I'm grateful.

When I was young, I think I gave up on life. I decided that it wasn't any fun and so I never had any. Now I'm ready to start living. For the first time in my life, I'm really feeling free. And that includes being free enough to share my life with somebody else. Since I no longer need to block my sexual feelings, I no longer need to push men away.

I haven't pictured the man I will marry yet, but I do know he will be gregarious and self-assured, and at least as strong as I. I'm ready for a powerful man because I'm no longer afraid he will control me.

*   *   *   *

When Ellen was a child, she made an equation: A relationship means sexual demands and sex hurts.

So what did she do? She grew up and played out her childhood script. Her husband, gynecologist and psychologist took the role of villain, confirming the fact that men want women strictly for sex. And Ellen obligingly accepted her part as the victim.

When she came to me, Ellen didn't like men. She was furious at them and was punishing them by denying her own sexuality. She had reached a point where she didn't even want to be in a relationship because that meant sex and she resented the pressures and expectations.

Because she was afraid of getting hurt like her mother, Ellen had built a vault around herself, refusing to give the key to the men in her life. She decided not to give them the only part of herself that she thought they wanted.

Soon after she agreed to make love, she grew bored with her affairs. And no wonder. As I see it, boredom is anger in disguise. Since Ellen didn't want a sexual relationship in the first place, her resentments piled up. She got bored, angry.

Think about the times when you were bored? Weren't you actually angry? Remember staring at the clock in English class and thinking that the teacher was boring you to death? Weren't you really angry that she was taking up your time and resentful because you had to be there in the first place?

Ellen had some old tapes to revise before she would be free to fall in love and enjoy a lasting relationship. She needed to allow herself, first of all, to like men. She had to believe that there are men who want women as whole people, not just sex objects. When she truly believed this, she would be free to start attracting that type.

In addition, she had to allow herself to enjoy her sexuality. Sex is fun and there's nothing wrong with having fun. A good relationship is one in which the partners care about each other; and one of the ways they express their feelings is through sex. They give and receive pleasure because both of them want to.

Sex isn't a command performance. And Ellen had to learn that it's okay to say no. If a man can't accept and respect her feelings, then he's not the right one for her anyway. There are plenty of men who are interested in more than a sexual fling. Ellen will find them as soon as she begins to believe they exist.

Too often, women endure sex because they feel they must. These are the women, I believe, who keep the gynecologists in business, because when their resentment festers, they end up with all kinds of vaginal infections. Their bodies are literally saying, "I don't want to be sexual" or "I'm afraid to be vulnerable."

Such women make easy prey for unethical therapists who take advantage of their clients' weakness. Unfortunately, such occurrences are amazingly common. It's important for women to be aware of this and say "no".

Although Ellen thought at the time that her psychologist had her best interests at heart, I believe that it's never okay for a therapist to have sexual relations with a client. A specially trained sex surrogate is a different story, but even in that case, sex is purely clinical and is performed only with the client's full consent and understanding of the goals. The kind of relationship Ellen had with her psychologist did more harm than good. The only purpose it served was to increase her confusion and guilt about sex.

Ellen's sexual feelings—or lack of them—are more common than you might think in our so-called "liberated" age. For one thing, there are still plenty of women who are virgins when they marry. You'd be surprised, too, at the number of young couples who don't consummate their marriage on their wedding night because they're either too scared or don't know what to do.

Often, they've been taught that sex is dirty and should be saved for marriage. When they finally get the piece of paper that makes it legal, they're supposed to forget everything they've felt and believed up until then. They're supposed to turn off the cold water and replace it immediately with hot. This is harder to do than it sounds, since our "plumbing" is connected to our feelings.

One possible solution is to experiment beforehand. I, for one, don't think we would have been given our sexual parts if we weren't meant to enjoy them. But sexuality is something we have to decide for ourselves.

Morality is what WE alone believe is right. Instead of doing what society or our parents or our religious leaders would have us do, I think we need to get in touch with our own feelings. We need to peel away the outside prejudices and the inside guilts to find out what WE want. Usually, I find that when I help clients do this, they pick a healthy pathway. People are basically good, I believe, and know right from wrong.

That doesn't mean because we decided sex is okay, it will automatically be good. Despite the limited sex education we get from our parents and teachers, most of us enter into our sexual relationships with little more than a basic knowledge of the physical fundamentals. We know nothing about the sensual pleasures involved in lovemaking. That's where communication comes in.

Couples need to learn to talk to each other and ask for what they want. As I see it, lovemaking is like ordering dinner in a fine restaurant. Most of us are not so presumptuous as to order for another person. Even if we knew what that person wanted yesterday, it might not be what he would like today.

And if that's true of food, it's even more important when it comes to making love. We're taught that it's not polite to ask for what we want. Does it make more sense to expect our partner to read our mind?

Expecting that almost always leads to problems because no one else can get inside our heads. Still, many of us mistakenly believe, "If you really loved me, you would *know* what I want." That's hogwash and can be dangerous to a relationship. The truth is, "I love you and that's why I want you to tell me what you desire."

Often in our relationships, we act like two ships sailing in a fog. The first thing we need to do is steer out of the fog by becoming clear on what we want. And then we need to take time to communicate with each other. More often than not, we will discover that we're both looking for the same things. Among them, love, caring and sharing, both verbally and physically.

Ellen has to tell the men in her life that she wants to get to know them before she's physically intimate with them. I'm sure she will discover that many men feel the same way, that there are lots of sensitive, caring men out there who are interested in more than a sexual relationship. With them, she'll have the chance to explore and enjoy her own sexuality and the healthy relationship she desires.

Chapter 8

Dwayne's Story:

BEING A SUCCESSFUL LAWYER DOESN'T
FIT MY IMAGE OF MYSELF

My resume was impressive—Harvard Law School, ten years experience as corporate counsel, last salary $55,000, married, no children, 40 years old—so why couldn't I find a job? Why was I grubbing alongside attorneys with half my qualifications?

Before I moved to California two years ago, I hadn't stopped to consider the employment prospects. I assumed that it would be relatively easy for a man of my experience to find a position with a major law firm. Boy was I wrong.

For one thing, there are even more attorneys in California than there are freeways. I have also discovered that it's rare for a law firm to hire a man my age; most prefer to promote from within.

I knocked on twenty or more doors before one partner finally agreed to hire me as an associate. But I ended up losing that job even before I started because of a political problem with the other associates. Talk about humiliation.

By the time I resumed my job search, I was bitter. "What's the use anyway?" I thought to myself. In desperation I took a job as a junior employee with a somewhat shaky small partnership.

The alternative was to start my own practice, but the thought of building a clientele terrified me. Besides, the financial risks would be substantial and the emotional ones even greater. I was afraid that after investing a tremendous amount of time and money, I'd end up failing. I wasn't sure I was good enough or sharp enough to make it on my own. Having my own practice didn't fit my image of myself.

So I chose to feel like a failure without ever trying. I was defeated because I felt defeated. Just look what other men my age have accomplished, I chided myself. Most lawyers are senior partners well before they reach 45; some are governors; John Kennedy was President of the United States. Obviously, I didn't have what it takes.

My self-esteem had hit rock bottom. My general outlook on life, for that matter, had always been grim. I grew up in New Jersey, the son of a struggling clothing salesman who suffered from diabetes. In the end he died of complications from the disease. He deserved more and I've always wondered if that's all there is to life.

Like my dad, I never considered myself a winner. As far back as grade school, I wasn't popular with the other kids. I didn't understand why since I was a very accommodating child, always willing to do what it took to please my classmates. But whatever I did, they never seemed to accept me.

When it came to sports, I was awful, a real whimp. I was always the last one picked for the baseball team, and then only because the teacher insisted that everyone play.

Since I was a failure at sports, I concentrated on my schoolwork instead. But getting good grades alienated me even more from my classmates. And the pain and embarrassment of not being accepted by my peers still haunts me.

When I finished high school, I entered a seminary to study for the priesthood. But I soon realized that a life of celibacy and complete regimentation wasn't for me. Instead, I joined the Peace Corps and spent two years in Peru. I still wanted to help people and it was a worthwhile experience.

At 25, I decided to return to school to study law. I'm not sure exactly why I chose this field, except that like the priesthood, it's a helping profession. I must admit there were other considerations as well. I wanted to be a respected professional, not just another man on the street. I wanted to be somebody.

Although I didn't do as well as I should have in law school, I did end up becoming a somebody. For ten years, I was a corporate counsel for a well-known New Jersey corporation. It was a secure, comfortable job until another company bought us out and began shaking up the place. When one of my friends five years my junior was promoted over me, I decided it was time to move on. That's when my wife and I took off for California.

The professional blow, compounded by my inability to find the kind of job I wanted in the Bay Area, was devastating. When I finally ended up in therapy, I felt like my shoes were glued to the pavement and there was nothing I could do to move.

I was miserable in my job but I didn't see any alternatives. Sure, intellectually I knew that nobody gives success to you, that only you can create it. But I couldn't seem to transfer that knowledge into practice. I was just plain stuck.

When I began working with visualizations, the same image recurred time after time: I was a chubby, gawky kid, and nobody wanted me for his baseball team. Although the situation might

54

seem insignificant now, it was mortifying to me as a child. I don't think there's anything more awful to a young person than being ignored or belittled by his peers.

The self-image that I didn't measure up, that I wasn't enough, followed me to adulthood. To change that image, Helene explained, I first had to visualize a new, positive experience.

So this time, I visualized myself being picked much sooner for the team. This time, I was good, really good. I hit a home run, and all the other little boys cheered and told me I was great.

Don't ask me how these creative imageries work. As a lawyer trained to deal with logic and facts, I can t explain them. All I know is that they helped me feel better about myself. With new information, I could change my original decisions and from there enhance my self-image. I decided that since I was acknowledged and accepted by my peers, I was enough.

In other visualizations, I discovered that the fears of money and responsibility were also holding me back. When I visualized money one day, an old proverb from the Bible popped into my head: "It's easier for a camel to get through the eye of a needle than for a rich man to get to heaven." Partly from my religious training, I assume, I felt that I shouldn't be so concerned about earning a good living. In reality, there's not a damn thing wrong with making money—except that wealth demands a certain amount of responsibility.

And responsibility is something else that scared me. It was humiliating for a supposedly sophisticated lawyer to admit this. But repeatedly in my guided imageries, I pictured the word "responsibility" written in enormous letters across the sky. They were scary.

Looking back, I see that I used to be too much of a perfectionist. I believed that everything I did had to turn out exactly right or it would prove that I was a failure. Since I couldn't handle that kind of responsibility, I usually didn't try in the first place. Helene helped me let go of being perfect, and then I was willing to take on more responsibility.

Could I then even picture myself as a successful lawyer? When Helene asked me to do this, I drew a blank. To me, a successful lawyer wears a three-piece, navy blue suit, works in a small-to-medium-sized firm, has lots of business, and is respected inside as well as outside the profession. Even now as I write this, I'm dressed in my own work clothes—a beige, two-piece suit.

Still, I believed I wanted to be a successful lawyer more than anything else in the world. I had to. After all, my father had spent all that money on law school, and I had invested so many years.

So, the next step was to visualize myself looking like a successful lawyer. I did, and I then made the affirmation, "I, Dwayne, am seeing myself as a successful lawyer." It worked, and I decided to take a chance on opening my own law office last year, although I still felt scared.

It was even rougher than I anticipated and I have been struggling to survive. Building a clientele hasn't been the most difficult part; learning to keep the books and worrying about paying the rent are worse. I haven't set the world on fire. I understand that it will take time, but I wonder if I'm still sabotaging myself because of a deep-rooted resistance to money.

The strange part is that now that I finally have a good chance to make it as a lawyer, I'm no longer sure that's what I want to do. I'm not as driven anymore. Now that I'm beginning to feel better about myself, more self-confident, I realize that there are all kinds of other options open to me.

I'm still searching. To make up my mind, I first have to figure out what I've been trying to prove and who I've been trying to please. If I'm going to make a mark on the world, I've decided it's going to be because I want to—not because I think I should, or have to prove something to myself and others, or because other people have done it.

I'm smart enough to realize that there's no blueprint for our lives; we create them the way we see them. Recently, my wife and I have been talking about creating a business together. There's a lot of power between the two of us.

What I'm beginning to realize is that I'm not my father; I'm me. I've had all kinds of advantages in life, partly because of my father's help. And there's every possibility that my life will be far more rewarding than his.

Intellectually, I've known for a long time that I alone am responsible for my destiny. I think I'm finally ready to accept that responsibility.

*   *   *   *

None of the other lawyers wanted him; it was the kids' baseball team all over again. Because none of Dwayne's schoolmates wanted him on their team, he believed that he didn't measure up, that he wasn't enough. He made the decision as a little boy that he'd never be as good as his peers. Succeeding academically only increased his sense of not belonging.

As unfair as it sounds, bright children are often rejected by their peers. They learn that success means pain and rejection. So they either block their intelligence or continue to do well in school at the price of feeling very isolated.

Possibly as a result of his earlier experiences with peer rejection, Dwayne blocked his intelligence and didn't do as well as he could have in law school. Also, he may have been acting out the decision that he wasn't good enough. And later at work, when his friend was promoted above him, the negative decision was reinforced once again.

So here he was, a qualified attorney who couldn't find a job. At 40 years old, he still couldn't make the team and his belief that he was not enough became a self-fulfilling prophesy.

Dwayne's feelings of inferiority aren't unusual. Most people are afraid that they're not good enough in certain areas. We react to this decision in different ways: Some people hold themselves back because they think it's useless to try. Others try to prove their success by driving themselves mercilessly. The problem is that although they may end up looking successful, they still don't feel like it inside.

Because Dwayne saw himself as a loser, he went to the opposite extreme to compensate. He decided to pursue law because it was a prestigious profession that would enable him to prove his worth. He wanted to show everyone that he was as good or better than they, that he wasn't a whimp.

But, at the same time, he held back because being a sophisticated lawyer didn't fit his image of himself. Unconsciously, he was still modeling himself after his father. He wasn't convinced that the son of a poor struggling salesman could end up a respected attorney.

Trying to prove to himself and everyone else that he was important was a losing battle. Dwayne found out the hard way that *we're not happy when we do something to prove anything*; we're only *happy when we do it because we want to.*

Even as a young boy, Dwayne did things to please other people. He was the typical placator, pleading, "I'll do anything you want; just like me." A placator, however, doesn't usually get the respect of his peers. For although some people may try to control others, they don't respect them if they can get away with it.

When I met Dwayne, he was depressed and furious. He felt trapped in a degrading job, and he was bitter about it. He was also bitter about the rejection he felt by his peers both as a child and an adult. He felt like a helpless victim who wasn't recognized or appreciated. Under all that, he was angry because his father worked so hard and got so little in return, and he himself seemed to be experiencing the same injustice.

This attitude was preventing Dwayne from doing what he really wanted to do with his life. He felt powerless and defeated before he even started.

He also seemed to be punishing himself by not allowing himself to be happy. Even in his job as corporate counsel, he admits now, he wasn't content. He settled for being safe rather than satisfied. Perhaps he felt guilty about leaving the priesthood and guilty because lawyers make big money.

Dwayne was, indeed, stuck. For him to take a risk on starting his own practice showed new courage. He's actually doing well, although he's still too hard on himself.

Like many people, he keeps looking at where he thinks he should be at 40, rather than appreciating and accepting where he is. He compares himself to the men his age who seem to have accomplished more, but he doesn't consider the ones who didn't make it to first base.

We all ask for pain when we use others as a yardstick to measure our own success. Instead, we need to look inside ourselves, find out where we are and where we want to go, then follow our own special path. *We have to allow ourselves to be not who we think we should be, but who we uniquely are.*

We need to appreciate ourselves for our little successes. Dwayne has had many. He is beginning, for example, to overcome some major stumbling blocks to his professional success, including his fear of responsibility, his resistance to making money, and his tendency to be extremely self-critical.

He's no longer paralyzed by his fear of responsibility. In fact, in one therapy session he saw those enormous letters in the sky shrink to a more manageable size. He realized that by putting responsibility into its proper perspective, he could handle it with confidence.

Money, too, is beginning to take on a new image for him, as Dwayne allows himself to spend it on pleasures like traveling and new clothes. Actually, I think money has an undeservedly bad reputation. Money is merely a piece of paper or a metal coin. It is powerless on its own; it's merely a tool. We alone give it the power to be good or bad. If we choose, we can use money to do all kinds of good things for ourselves and other people. Dwayne had to let go of the feeling that pious, good people should not want money.

Learning to deal with his critical parent was another important step towards Dwayne's happiness. The critical parent is that part of ourselves that shakes a pointed finger at us and tells us what we *should* do or feel in order to be okay. Dwayne was so busy listening to his "shoulds" that he had little time for his wants.

Each of us has within our subconscious a critical parent. To get in touch with yours, you might try one of the exercises that helped Dwayne. Close your eyes and picture your critical parent in front of you. That person might look like one of your own parents, yourself, or even a witch. First, hear what he or she is telling you to do, and then make your own decision. Say, "I hear what you're telling me, and I want to do ____, and I am okay."

Sometimes, your critical parent will be right—"You should go to your doctor for a checkup," and "You should use your seatbelt." When you agree with the opinion, follow it. When you don't agree, realize that you are free to do what you want, and you are okay.

Dwayne figured that he should be a lawyer because he had worked so hard to be one. He felt he had to prove to himself and his peers that he could make it. When he no longer feels he has to prove anything, he will be free to decide what he wants.

Maybe after he convinces himself that he is a good lawyer, he will choose to do something else. The point is that he now realizes he has options. When Dwayne put all his "shoulds" into the proper perspective, he allowed himself the freedom to begin exploring other career possibilities.

Sure, taking a chance on anything new can be terrifying. But so what? The next time you want to move on but are scared to do so, ask yourself, "What is the worst thing that can happen if I go for it?" Then ask, "What's worse than that? And what's even worse than that?" Most of the time, your goal will be worth the risks. You might find that the only thing worse than moving on is staying where you are.

For Dwayne, the trauma of switching careers might be less than remaining in the legal profession. He's wise to ask himself if there's another profession that would give him more satisfaction. Although it might be less prestigious, it might offer other rewards.

Personally, I believe Dwayne may never be totally happy with his present career; I don't think it fulfills enough of his unique potential. He loves to help people and perhaps he will find a way to do so more to his satisfaction.

Meanwhile, he's letting go of the remaining negative thoughts that are preventing him from moving on. As Dwayne explores his uniqueness and realizes that he can be whatever he wants to be, he is finding his own pathway to happiness and success.

Chapter 9 ⎯⎯⎯⎯⎯⎯⎯⎯⎯

Susan's Story:

MUSICAL SUCCESS MEANS PAIN

I used to read music like other teenagers read romance novels. My favorite "authors" were Tchaikovsky and Rachmaninoff, and the piano was my life.

As a child, I believed that I'd grow up to be the best pianist in the world. I dreamed about composing music for an entire orchestra and conducting it myself. It's hard to believe that something so wonderful could end up bringing me so much pain.

I discovered the piano when I was 4 years old. I was intrigued by one in a restaurant, and I just sat down and started playing a tune I'd once heard on the radio. Soon after that, my father bought a piano and signed me up for lessons. I think I was the happiest little girl in the world. I slept, ate and breathed music. I even thought in musical notes; there was always some unpublished symphony kicking around in my brain.

I played by ear until I was 10 and learned to read music. I practiced up to ten hours a day, including at least two hours of scales. They gave me a high that joggers say they get from running.

By the time I was 13, I could memorize a 14 page composition. But although I could handle anything that had to do with music, I wasn't as lucky with my homelife. There I was a failure, and I felt powerless to do anything about it.

My mother died when I was born; my father and older aunt raised me. I adored my aunt and I would entertain her with my music for hours.

Dad was a different story. He didn't have time to listen; he didn't give a hoot about me. When he wasn't busy working, he was out with his girlfriends. When he was home, it was worse. When he had one of his frequent headaches, he would walk around the house slamming doors and throwing things and even beat my aunt and me. All he did was fight with us. He would bait my aunt until she was in tears, and it only made things worse when I tried to defend her. I was a nobody—just a child.

I tried my best to practice piano in this atmosphere but it was virtually impossible. Oh, how I wished my father would learn to love my music as much as I did. If he would just listen, I knew I could make him happy.

At 16, I gave my first major recital. Dad said he'd rather die than miss it and I was in heaven. When Sunday finally came, I was so excited I couldn't sit still.

I started my first piece, then turned around to smile at my dad. But to my horror, his seat was empty. I felt a stabbing pain through my heart. Somehow, I made it through the next two pieces and even got a standing ovation. But when I stood up to thank the audience, I almost collapsed from hurt and anger. I was devastated because I couldn't impress the one person in the world I wanted to please the most.

After my recital, I was invited to perform on radio. I knew I was on the road to the top and yet I felt like I was sliding backwards too fast to stop. The fights at home were worse than ever and I knew I'd have to give up my dreams. My music career was crashing down around me.

Saying goodbye to it was like losing a child. Everytime I listened to the radio, I cried with grief. Without my one love in life, I decided that life wasn't worth living.

Other than my aunt, I had nobody to confide in. My father wouldn't let me have any friends. I was unbelievably lonely and didn't know where to turn.

I ended up with a married man I'd met on the street. I didn't know beans about sex, and so I decided to learn from experience. The result was a messy vaginal infection which I chose to ignore rather than admit to my father.

I could see no way out of my predicament, and I made up my mind one night to leave this cruel world by swallowing a bottle of pills. The last thing I remember that day is taking the pills and drifting off.

When I woke up, I couldn't wait to find out what heaven looked like. I was sure it would be filled with Baby Grand pianos. Just imagine my shock and despair when I opened my eyes to find myself in my very own bedroom.

My dad took me to the doctor and she diagnosed my venereal disease. When she told Dad about it, he was all apologetic and lovey dovey.

But it didn't last. Before long, he was throwing my mistake up to me, calling me a bitch, slut and whore. That did it. I slammed the door on our relationship, deciding that I would never again trust him.

I thought about running away. I even considered becoming a prostitute. Instead, I got married when I was barely 18 to a man who turned out to be a real bastard. Before I finally gave birth to our two children, my husband gave me two miscarriages by kicking me in the stomach.

Life was still hell and I didn't even have a piano for solace. Paul didn't want one in the house. One day I decided I'd had enough; I took the children to the park and never returned home.

I call my second marriage my legal love affair. I loved sex and Joe and I spent the better part of our time together in bed. Because he didn't want me to work, I quit my job as a store manager and stayed home. Although I had a piano again, I seldom touched it, especially when anyone was around. An audience terrified me. Even when I tried to play for small family parties, I fell apart.

While I was home, I learned to crochet and knit and became the perfect housewife. My children looked like they had just finished a Tide commercial and I was miserable. Even our sex life had fizzled. After Joe taught me everything he knew, I still wanted to learn more. But, to my horror, he ended up impotent. One night, he got so frustrated he tried to kill me. That marriage ended in my second divorce.

I met my present husband, Marvin, four years ago. One night, he asked what I wanted to do with my life and for five hours, I rambled on about music. "If you ever want to see me again," Marvin told me in the morning, "You have to go back to your music."

I was petrified. Everytime something good happened to me, it was taken away. I had buried my music for 20 years and I couldn't bear to lose it for the second time.

I decided finally that the emptiness inside me was worse than taking the chance. And somehow I found the courage to try again. I enrolled in music school and I married Marvin. I was so happy that I was miserable. "You're not good enough; you don't deserve this," I thought to myself. I was terrified that something would spoil it all.

The thought of playing for anyone else, even my husband and children, still sent me into a panic. And there was always someone around the house, and another excuse for not practicing.

For one thing, the old piano sounded dreadful. I needed a new one, and I fantasized about buying a Baby Grand. Too bad that it wouldn't fit in our living room, and too bad we couldn't afford one even if it did.

When I decided to go to Helene for therapy, I was more depressed than ever. I was doing poorly in school and I couldn't get myself to practice or study. To get me through the day, I was taking tranquilizers prescribed by a doctor.

Fortunately, the creative visualization process started working immediately. In a very powerful session, I visualized that awful Sunday recital that my father had missed. Although I'd never realized it before, I had decided at that moment that music was too painful to continue.

After I released the old pain in Helene's office, I created a new scene. This time, my dad was sitting in the front row, applauding and looking at me with pride and respect.

In other visual exercises, I substituted the turmoil at home for tranquility. Instead of my father slamming doors and beating me, he was quiet and kind.

Now, Helene asked me, "See the person you want to be." In my imagination, I saw an extremely powerful person and it scared the daylights out of me. The power of my music had always disturbed me. As a little girl, I was meek and powerless; power didn't fit my image. Expressing myself again through my music was like putting my finger into an electrical outlet; it sent shivers through my body.

So I started working on a new self-image, re-owning my power. I pictured myself playing piano in front of hundreds of people who loved my music. And I saw myself standing up to my father, telling him how important music was to me, and explaining why I needed a comfortable atmosphere in which to practice. This time he agreed with me and did everything he could to encourage my talent. In my visualization, my father returned my love and I saw myself become a strong, self-assured person with some powerful messages to give to the world through music.

I was beginning to feel better about myself and more optimistic about life. One day Marvin took me into a music store to measure a Baby Grand. It would fit in our living room! The next thing I knew, he was writing a check.

Three days later, I sat down and played a song for my wonderful husband. It sounded beautiful. Musicians must have good instruments in order to do a good job. I began to recognize something in my music that I hadn't heard in years.

Since then my skill has been improving daily. I barely have to study for my classes and I'm getting A's. A few weeks ago, I offered to play a song for my professor. To my surprise, I was as comfortable as when I used to play for my auntie, and it felt good.

Thanks to Marvin, I'm getting the chance to start my life over. Perhaps I would have found my way back to music eventually, but Marvin helped it happen sooner.

I truly love the man. Marvin is an honest-to-goodness friend. I can work with him, play with him, and cry with him. We love with a love that's strong and true and lasting, even though I don't see rockets when we make love.

At one time, sex was uppermost in my life. Now music is far more important. You might say that I've reached a point of no return. Reclaiming my music is like welcoming my child back from the dead. This time I'm going to nourish and cherish it. I'm not going to hide anymore behind an apron of fright.

I have a message to give to the world; it's time I had the courage to share it. With my music back, I like life and everything about the vitality of living. Now that I've overcome my Fear of Success, I'm enjoying my music and I'm thrilled to share it with everyone who will listen.

*   *   *   *

We all have a unique talent. If we don't use our gift, we experience a gnawing feeling inside: A part of us wants to emerge, and we're not totally happy until we express it.

What a shame it would have been if Susan never shared her music, her special gift to the world! Until now, her Fear of Success stopped her. As a child, she learned to associate her musical success with pain. Not only did her father repeatedly interrupt her practice, but he also failed to show up for the all-important recital.

Susan never again wanted to be hurt like that. So to block that pain, she blocked her musical ability. Unfortunately, she cut off a big part of herself, the part that made her feel alive and excited about life.

Because she didn't see a way out of her pain, she tried to kill herself. *Suicide is a symptom saying, "Help, I can't take the pain anymore."*

Unable to bear such pain, thousands of people take their own lives each year. Thousands of others unconsciously choose what I call "legal suicide." When they believe that life is no longer worth living, they may end up in a terrible car crash or with a serious disease. Even so, I don't believe they really want to kill themselves; they just want to stop the pain.

My question is, "How do you know that death will stop the hurt?" Nobody knows.

When clients threaten suicide, I ask if they'd want to live if they felt less pain. Virtually all of them say yes, and so we work on releasing the pain and feeling better. And then they go on living.

Most likely, Susan's father was in too much pain himself to be there for his daughter. As a result, all her efforts to please him were in vain.

Many of us spend our lives trying to please Mom and Dad. That's why it's so important for parents to let their children know how much they love and appreciate them no matter how old they are.

I believe some parents make a mistake by not encouraging talent such as Susan's. Usually they think they're doing their children a favor by pushing them towards more practical, secure, better-paying careers. I have a client who is a car mechanic and hates his job; he always dreamed of being a poet.

While it's wise for parents to guide their children towards a skill that will support them, it's also important to encourage their unique creative potential. Otherwise, their children will always feel like they're missing something. A balanced person can be both practical and idealistic, a mechanic and a poet, an executive and a pianist.To feel complete and whole, we need to express all our parts.

Susan felt powerless to do this. She had always felt weak next to her father; she was afraid that he would hurt her if she expressed herself.

When I asked her to visualize her power, it scared her. True power enables us to express ourselves; and subconsciously, Susan was afraid that if she released that energy, she might misuse it.

Re-owning her power meant she would have to give up her victim role, which had become so familiar and comfortable. When you re-own your power, you also take on the responsibility that goes with it. Often, people resist giving up the old role because they don't want to take responsibility for themselves. If they did, they would have nobody to blame if something went wrong.

It seemed safer for Susan to stay with what she knew. Twice she had married men just like her father. Children of abusive parents often believe that they don't deserve better. If Susan's husbands had treated her nicely, she probably would have pushed them away. It didn't fit her image of herself.

As a woman, Susan believed that she didn't deserve much from a relationship; and as a musician, she felt she didn't merit a good piano. One common way we keep ourselves stuck is by using inferior instruments or tools. We feel we don't deserve the best unless we reach a certain level of achievement or success. We don't realize that we might reach that level sooner if our tools weren't holding us back. Susan believed she wasn't good enough for a Baby Grand; when she got it, however, her music improved dramatically.

We do ourselves a favor by investing in the best we can. Strangely enough, there's often a difference between what we think we can afford and what we can actually afford. For instance, we usually find the money to buy what's important to us or what we're willing to allow ourselves to buy. It's a matter of deciding what will make us feel good about ourselves and then setting priorities.

I'm not suggesting that you add to the national debt, only that you make some conscious choices. Are you spending your money on what you really want? Or are you spending it on what you think you should? Or only on what you feel you deserve?

Susan made the mistake of ignoring her needs. Because she stifled her music, she felt empty inside. She tried to fill the void by redirecting her creative energy into sexual energy.

At the same time, she was looking for a man who would give her all the love that she felt her father had withheld. But it didn't work because love comes from the heart and not the sex organs. Each affair left her as empty as before and to fill that emptiness, she needed one "fix" after another. She became a "sexaholic."

With the sexual demands she placed on her husbands, it's no wonder that one of them became impotent. Impotency is often saying, "I'm scared" or "I'm angry or resentful." Frequently, it's a fear of emotional castration. It might mean, "I'm afraid to give to you" or "I don't want to." Women who don't enjoy sex may be feeling the same thing.

For Susan, sex couldn't make up for the music she so desperately missed. It's interesting that when she was finally ready to pursue her music again, she created a man in her life who really cared about her and her special talent.

Ironically, she now appears to be holding back her sexuality. A part of her may still believe that she doesn't deserve to enjoy both her sexuality and her music. For a long time, she was afraid that if she felt too good, something bad would happen.

That lingering fear of getting hurt is her final hurdle. When she clears it, she will surely realize that she deserves to have it all.

Chapter 10

Robert's Story:

MY PARENTS WON'T LOVE ME IF
I'M HAPPIER THAN THEY ARE

All my life I've been waiting for happiness to strike and to fill me with a sense of well-being.

I used to blame my unhappiness on my body. You see, through an awful mistake in genes, I believe I was born Baby Girl Roberta instead of Baby Robert. Ever since I can remember, I've felt like a boy unfairly trapped inside a female's body. I'd stare in the mirror at my long braids and budding breasts and wish desperately that I'd been born with a penis instead. I wanted more than anything else in the world to be what I felt I truly was.

In my heart I knew that somehow someday I would be a man. And I was convinced that my life wouldn't begin until that moment.

As soon as I turned 21, I checked into the hospital to begin my transformation. With the help of hormones, my voice dropped and hair began appearing on my face. Then I went through a series of operations, including a mastectomy, hysterectomy and plastic surgery.

The whole process took close to five years, but, finally, I could present myself to the world the way I'd always believed I should be.

So why was I still in so much pain? Why was life still dumping on me, just like my mother warned it would? Why was I still waiting for the joy that always seemed to evade my family?

Ours was an oppressively unhappy household. My mother was a gloom and doomer, who believed that everything just naturally turned out awful. She'd had an unhappy childhood herself, and her favorite expressions were "poor me," "poor you" and "isn't that terrible." For every small rainbow, she'd point out the rainstorm.

Although she might have acted like a very weak person, she was in fact extremely powerful. Being the underdog gave her the power she needed; she ruled by guilt. And, oh, my four brothers and I became so good at accepting the burden of that guilt.

Mother was the martyr; we were the poor Christians she appointed herself to save from the lion's den of life. She sacrificed everything for us. After she divorced her first husband, an alcoholic, Mother married my father "for the kids' sake." After that, she stayed in the marriage "because I need a man to help support you children."

Actually, she hated my father and managed to turn us all against him, too. Although he probably didn't deserve such disrespect, it's true that he couldn't hold down a job. He just dreamed about being someone important, while Mother worked to support us and focused all her attention on her children.

Neither of them knew how to show affection. Ironically, Dad ended up physically abusing the very children he was supposed to rescue. Once he nearly killed my brother over something so minor I can't even remember what it was. I guess because I was the only girl, I escaped most of the physical abuse. And that just added to the rest of my guilts.

My brothers and I were never particularly close. My parents kept us apart. In turn, each one of us felt like the unimportant one, the only one who wasn't getting a share of love. I, for one, was convinced that it was me. As a girl, I felt like odd person out.

It was a lonely existence since we'd been taught that the family was supposed to be not only the center of our universe but its boundaries as well. Mother warned us not to trust outsiders, and we were forbidden to bring our schoolmates home with us.

I didn't know how to have any fun, and I wasn't convinced that it was possible anyway. Even as I got older, I didn't date. I was a physical and emotional misfit, after all, so who would have me? To ease the pain, I turned to drugs but, of course, they didn't help.

Then, one day, I decided that I wanted to be a rabbi—no small task for a young lady who wasn't even Jewish. It was the healthy family emphasis, I think, that most attracted me. I can't say that I'm the least bit religious; even now, I see myself as an atheist. I came up with the idea of converting when we studied in school about the Jewish people and concentration camps. Looking back, I wonder if I, too, wasn't playing martyr by attempting to take on the weight of the whole persecution.

Anyway, one day I bound my chest, pretended I was a boy, and headed off to join a religious school. To no one's surprise, it didn't work out and I landed back home with Mother.

For awhile, joining a theater group helped give some meaning to my boring life. Again, I pulled in my chest and passed myself off as a young boy. I was a natural for the stage; after all, I had been role-playing all my life.

But I was getting tired of this cross-living, not to mention the fact that my mother was driving me crazy. She felt that she must have done something awful for me to do this to her, and she never missed an opportunity to beat her breast and tell me so.

Despite the emotional beating I managed to give myself, I still believed that a sex-change operation was my only chance for happiness, and I decided to go through with it. I was working at the time as a chem lab assistant and my medical insurance covered most of the hospital bills.

When it was over, I was pleased with the results. I liked being a man; I couldn't imagine being anyone else. But something was still missing. I had everything that I'd always believed I wanted, and yet I continued to feel empty, unfulfilled. I was still waiting for happiness to strike.

While I wallowed in my unhappiness, I remained at home with Mom and the three brothers who hadn't yet married. My father had split when I was 16, and we felt Mother, who had developed a serious illness, needed us. Don't ask me why, but I think I felt responsible for her failing health. I also felt responsible for paying a good share of the rent, since my older brothers didn't have steady jobs and couldn't help out. I was playing martyr, just like my poor mother. I had learned my lessons well.

I hope that doesn't sound too bitter. Actually, I don't mean to present her as a horrible person bent on hurting others. Any harm she may have caused, I really believe, was done innocently. I know she did the best she could.

Sometimes, though, I felt so much hatred that I wanted to die. I didn't hate anyone in particular, but everyone, including my mother and myself.

The emptiness was destroying me by the time I decided to try some psychological therapy. Actually, it took me a long time to get up the courage. I think I was afraid to face myself. What if I had made a mistake in becoming a transsexual? It was too late to turn back now. Though I deeply believe I did what I had to do, that question occasionally still nags at me. I wonder whether being the only girl in the family made me feel insignificant as a female. Or maybe I was afraid that all women were as unhappy as my mother.

It was with these misgivings that I faced that first group therapy session. Would I be able to be honest? Would they think me a freak?

My fears turned out to be unfounded, and I learned some very important lessons in that group. Sure, people are different; but their problems are not. During the year of group therapy, the participants continued to change, but the problems and insecurities remained the same. Mine weren't so different from anyone else's.

I spent hours getting to know the frightened kid inside of me. But, despite all the work, I couldn't convince that unhappy little girl to go with me and be happy. Neither could I kill her off. Finally in one visualization, I decided to leave her with my mother. These two unhappy people would be excellent company.

The next step was to visualize my mother and father as loving, nurturing parents, encouraging me to be happier than they were. But again, the visualization was impossible. Instead, I adopted a new set of parents, ones who could give me all the love and care I needed, ones who would support my success. I made the affirmation, "I, Robert, am beginning to believe that my parents want me to be as happy and as successful as I can be."

That accomplished, I moved on to another visual exercise in which I met my "wise person," the knowledgable, insightful part of myself. I had to re-own that part, Helene explained, in order to set some goals.

Since I've always put such little importance on my own needs (something I learned from my mother), it's extremely difficult to decide what I do want. Through my indecision, I constantly sabotage myself. I start all kinds of projects at the same time, then worry about completing them. I usually don't.

I've learned from Helene that my inability to make up my mind and set goals and priorities is a result of a deep-rooted belief that I'm not good enough and so I don't deserve much. I'm working on changing that opinion.

Unfortunately, in my more painful moments, I think about all the failures in my family, and I'm scared that the same fate awaits me. I've never consciously thought that my parents won't love me if I'm more successful or happier than they were. But I have discovered in my unconscious that I do feel guilty for seeking that happiness.

That's when I remind myself that other people make it on their own strength, that my life is not dependent on the success or failure of my family. Only I am responsible for my happiness. And they are responsible for their misery or successes.

If I choose not to, I don't have to sacrifice myself like my mother. My unhappiness is not going to make her happier anyway.

Last year at 30 years old, I finally found the courage to move out of her house and into a home of my own. She didn't even lay a guilt trip on me; she couldn't because I wouldn't let her. I knew I was doing the right thing for me.

When I think back, I can't believe that I stayed in that depressing place for so long. Mother's power was so incredible. Her negativity filled every corner of the house and swallowed us up. Thank goodness I was finally able to find the strength I needed to break the pattern.

Not long after that, I met a wonderful, warm, loving girl. For the first time in my life, I made love. I'm not physically perfect as a man—my new apparatus doesn't perform as well as the real thing—but it didn't matter. That relationship helped me overcome my biggest fear, that I wouldn't be lovable to either sex.

After a whirlwind romance, we broke up. Sure, the split was traumatic, but I didn't get into a lot of self-damnation and guilt. Instead, I simply realized that I wasn't ready for something more permanent.

Today, I'm enjoying the luxury of having my own apartment. I'm also starting to re-own my happy kid. I'm learning to relax and play, to indulge myself in the small things that give me pleasure. Because my parents didn't know how to enjoy themselves, I learned early that playing was a waste of time. I'm only now starting to realize that I don't have to do something "productive" all the time.

That doesn't mean I'm slacking off at work. In fact, I'm doing very well. I've even returned to school to improve my skills. My grade-point average so far is 4.0.

I'm not sure what I want to be doing ten or even five years from now. I've got dozens of hobbies, and maybe I will eventually turn one into a career. Meanwhile, I'm proving to myself that I can be successful despite the shortcomings of the rest of my family.

I'm not going to sacrifice myself to negativity any longer. I certainly wasn't helping my mother by trying; I was just destroying myself along with her.

I've decided not to wait any longer for happiness to come to me on a magic carpet. It's high time that I myself started creating all I can!

*　　　*　　　*　　　*

Although Robert's sex change operation is rare, his problems are surprisingly common. Many people who are struggling with Fear of Success have an unconscious fear that if they're more successful than their parents, they will lose Mom and Dad's love. Logically, I admit, this fear doesn't make sense, and my clients are always startled to discover it.

But deep in their subconscious their kid often believes, "I'm the child and my parents should have more than I." Like Robert, many of my clients believe, "It's not fair for me to succeed where my parents have failed. They have struggled and suffered so much, so why should I have it so easy?" And in their visualizations, they hear that same message from their parents.

Robert's mother was too scared to be alone, so she stayed in an unhappy marriage. She really believed that she was doing it for the children's sake. Despite the staggering divorce rate today, you'd be surprised how many parents misguidedly stay together for this reason. Unfortunately, the situation often backfires, as it did in this case. Because Robert felt guilty for causing his parents' suffering, he ended up sabotaging his own happiness.

How sad and ironic that so many people react just like him. In truth, our parents would probably like nothing more than for us to be richer, happier and more successful than they.

Look at your own mother and father. Aren't they happiest when they can brag about you? "Did you know my son got a promotion? Have you seen pictures of my daughter's beautiful children? Did you know that the kids are vacationing this year in Europe?"

The greatest gift we can give our parents is to be the best we can possibly be!

Blinded by guilt, Robert couldn't see this. For years, his mother ruled the family with continual "shoulds" and negativity, and her children built their lives around the theme of suffering.

When people are hurting, they do incredible things to avoid their pain. They join religious cults, drown themselves in alcohol or drugs and, yes, maybe even go to such extremes as changing their sex. I'm not saying that Robert underwent a sex-change operation for the wrong reasons. I don't know; I didn't have the opportunity to counsel him while he still had the choice.

Neither am I blaming Robert's mother for his pain. *We alone are responsible for our decision to feel good or bad.* We base our reactions on our experiences regardless of who creates them. And our reactions are as varied as our individual personalities.

Consider for a moment the gas crisis back in the '70s. Remember the long lines at the pumps and how drivers dealt with them? Some people busted a gut; some sat patiently and read a book or polished their nails, and still others took the opportunity to sell lemonade and T-shirts. Notice, one situation with countless different responses.

This freedom of response is the reason siblings often grow up to be so different from one another. We each pick our own defenses. One child grows up thinking, "I'll show them. I'll succeed just to spite them." The other says, "You don't want me to succeed, so I won't." And still a third decides, "You want me to be successful and I'm angry at you. So there's no way I'm going to succeed."

Robert's mother, an extremely unhappy woman, spent her life feeling guilty. Her mother passed it on to her, and so she passed it on to her own children. But the children had the option of turning it down. *No one can make you feel guilty unless you choose to do so.* There's no sale unless someone's willing to buy.

Instead of buying into all the guilt, Robert is learning to trust his own feelings. He needs to stop punishing himself for the way his mother feels. She feels bad simply because she feels bad. Robert isn't the cause. When he decided to have his operation, his mother could have felt happy for him. She could have felt relieved. Instead, she chose to feel unhappy, and that was her decision alone.

Guilt is a "should." It says we should do, feel or think a certain way or we're not okay—we're wrong or bad.

Guilt is a learned response; it comes from parents, society, teachers and peers. It is *their* opinion. If we live life by guilt, we are not running our own life; we're letting everyone else do it for us.

To take charge of ourselves and our life, we need to ask ourselves what *we* feel, think or want to do. Then we must believe that we are okay for doing so. *We are the only ones who feel our pain or our joy, so we are the only ones who can decide what is right or wrong for us.*

Try this experiment: First say, "I should." Notice the way your body feels when you say it. Does it feel tense? Now say, "I want." How does your body feel this time? Is it more relaxed?

Guilt is not only unproductive but destructive to us as well as the people around us. It is a heavy, paralyzing burden. When we punish ourselves, we feel resentful. And so we end up hurting those we care about and want to help.

Instead, we need to give ourselves permission to follow our wants. To allow ourselves to do so is to be self-caring, rather than selfish. If we are good to ourselves, we will be free to give to others.

Because Robert and his brothers felt too guilty to leave their mother alone (after all, she gave up her life for them), they lived at home long after it was appropriate for them to build lives of their own. With this guilt came the inevitable resentment. And since they resented staying home, they unconsciously added to their mother's misery. Their life together became a vicious circle with no winners.

To break away from this cycle, Robert had to release his pain, anger, fear and sadness. Then, in the security of my office, he went through an entire rebirthing process. He envisioned himself leaving his family and floating through the universe to select a new set of loving, nurturing parents. After he found them, he settled back into the womb, feeding on the pure energy and love flowing from the umbilical cord. He heard his parents say how much they wanted him, and he felt good.

Then, when he was ready, he allowed himself a perfect birth. Similarly, he recreated the different stages of his growth. He saw himself being one of the boys, later joining the football team, and finally falling in love with a woman who loved him too.

Although this exercise was particularly valuable to Robert

because of his sex-change operation, it is not unique to him. This way of rebirthing is an important part of the therapy process for all of my clients who need to see and experience their lives in a positive, nurturing way.

In the process, Robert saw himself receiving the unconditional love and acceptance he needed from parents who loved each other. Because he felt loved, he was able to feel lovable.

His scared kid began to believe that it was okay to experience love outside the family. Eventually, he began to believe that he could have a fulfilling relationship with a woman. I wasn't surprised when he met a woman and made love to her. He had already visualized it in my office, and it was time for him to actualize it in real life.

This satisfying sexual relationship was a major step in Robert's progress. I believe that we all create the experiences we need to grow. We learn what we're supposed to learn from a particular situation or person, and then we need to move on.

Robert needed that sexual relationship to prove to himself that he could be a "real man." How many men have to prove that fact to themselves! The truth is, however, that no woman can make a man feel like that for an extended period of time. In order to be long-lasting and real, the belief has to come from within.

So Robert is continuing to work on re-owning himself. Part of that is learning to relax and play. He learned from his mother that it was virtuous to work but nobody taught him the importance of fun. Early on, many of us are indoctrinated with the virtue of hard work. But playing is something we may have to teach ourselves. Today, Robert is taking time to play racquetball, paint, and program his computer.

Play is a way of re-energizing our minds and bodies, releasing our tension, and making life more exciting and fun. It's this balance between work and play that makes us healthy. Notice how a vacation rejuvenates you and allows you to work even more efficiently?

Try a little experiment. Do something nice for yourself today simply because it feels good and you deserve it. Take a leisurely bubblebath, go dancing, buy something special for yourself or enjoy finishing this book.

Chances are that you'll feel better about facing the world tomorrow. Remember, it's okay for you to be happy, even happier than your parents. *Happiness is your birthright.* And watching you claim it just might make your parents smile.

Chapter 11_____

Rose's Story:

I'M AFRAID TO TAKE CHARGE OF MY LIFE
BECAUSE I'VE NEVER DONE IT BEFORE
AND I'M AFRAID OF THE UNKNOWN

Sometimes, I get so frustrated that I feel like screaming until my throat aches. But that's ridiculous. I can't scream; I can't even talk normally.

My speech problem started ten years ago without any warning. One morning, I woke up as usual beside my third husband and was shocked to discover that I couldn't utter an intelligible word.

Since then, I've been to all kinds of doctors but none of them can find a physical cause for my slurred, garbled speech. I hate sounding like this. You can't imagine the embarrassment I feel when I'm forced to talk to strangers. I'm sure they all think I'm either retarded or drunk.

It's obvious that as long as I have this problem I won't be able to do all the things I'd like to do with my life. Take a job, for instance. I've always dreamed about going into public relations, but who ever heard of a public relations person who can't talk?

I'm not proud of the way my life has gone up until now. No one brags about four marriages or repeated bouts with alcoholism.

Surprisingly, I started out as a very bright child. I was my mother's favorite; the cute, smart one. I loved my mother. I confided in her about everything. I sought her advice constantly, and I tried to follow it to the letter. Although she constantly criticized me and wanted me to do better, she loved me, too. That made it doubly important for me to please her.

I came to depend on that comfortable security and later sought the same kind of protection from the men in my life. When I married my first husband, I was a 16-year-old virgin. He turned out to be a selfish jerk. But I didn't know better and ended up producing three kids in rapid succession. The marriage was a mistake from the beginning, and I paid for it with migraine headaches. After eight years of pain, I decided to give up and get a divorce.

Meanwhile, just like in the movies, I had fallen in love with the doctor who had been treating my headaches. He became husband number 2, and for a time, the prestige of being married to a doctor was enough to make me happy. He is the father of my fourth child.

But my doctor made housecalls, and not all of them were professional. It wasn't long before I got fed up with his philandering, and in three years, I was divorced again.

The sad truth was that I couldn't live without a man. I needed the security and I needed a father for my kids. Husband number 3 was my biggest mistake. Jealous and possessive, he accused me constantly of having affairs with every man I met.

An attractive dress or a casual glance at another man was enough to throw him into a jealous rage. He would drink too much, then he would squeeze my cheeks until they turned black and blue.

The morning I woke up to find myself speechless, my husband, Nick, went to work as usual. He didn't care one bit about me. As for myself, I was convinced that my mysterious malady was punishment for yet another disastrous marriage.

By this time, Nick had traded his drinking problem for religion. He'd joined one of those cult churches where they put Christ's words to Nazi music. Although he tried to convert me, I wouldn't have any part of it. I offered him a choice between the church and me and I lost.

Meantime, I had been laid off from my job on an electronics company assembly line. I can't tell you how many doors were slammed in my face in the next few weeks. I was obviously losing control of my life and I turned to alcohol as an escape from my miseries.

Alcoholism is a disease and I believed that I "caught" it from my dad. Ever since I can remember, he was an alcoholic. I hated him when he came home drunk and embarrassed me in front of my friends. Even when he wasn't drunk, he often slurred his words; the doctors blamed it on a stroke.

Now, here I was, an alcoholic who literally couldn't talk her way out of a bottle, embarrassing my own kids in front of their friends. After seven very lonely years, I once again divorced and moved back in with Mom.

My mother was always there when I needed her. Boy, did I need her. She was 98 dependable pounds of dynamite and she encouraged my dependency. Poor me fell right into the trap; after all, it was easier to turn the reins of my life over to her than to gallop off on my own.

Looking back, I think she lavished all her attention on me

because she was unhappy with her own life. She once told me that she married my dad on the rebound, after her own parents refused to allow her to marry the man she really loved.

But living home again was a drag, and I was soon ready for husband number 4. He turned out to be my sister's ex-husband. Now don't jump to conclusions. While Arnold was married to my sister, there was never any funny business between us. We were just good friends. But after their divorce, we ran into each other again and began dating.

We were married four years ago and I moved south to be with him. The two children who were still in school begged to stay on with my mother and although I was hurt and felt guilty about shirking my responsibility, I gave in.

On my wedding day, I got plastered; my excuse was the celebration. But everyday I had another excuse. In the morning I would drink to get me started. In the afternoon, a drink would pick me up. When Arnold had a drink to unwind after work, I would join him with three or four.

Arnold is a kind, compassionate, wonderful man, who does everything he can to make me happy. But, I hate to admit, even he wasn't enough to sober me up. I was making myself miserable, and he couldn't do anything to help.

At work one day, I slipped and broke my neck. I was in agony, in a back brace for three months. When the doctor took me off medication, booze remained to relieve the pain.

But the emotional pain was even greater. Finally, I agreed to check into an alcohol rehabilitation hospital, and for several months, I stayed sober.

But my problems remained. I was still extremely self-conscious about my speech impediment. Although I was making some progress, it wasn't fast enough. My new job, too, was a source of trauma. I had been promoted to a position where I had to deal directly with the public, and it scared me to death. On top of all that, my father died about that time—just keeled over with a beer in his hands after an argument with me.

The excuses were plenty, and soon I was back to the bottle. I started nipping at lunch, and the guilt was tremendous. To drown it, I drank even more, working myself up to as much as a quart a day. One day in an insane effort to get some rest, I swallowed a handful of tranquilizers with a glass of vodka. Arnold had to call the paramedics and I eventually ended up back in rehab. That was a year ago, and I'm happy to report that I haven't touched a drop since.

But I'm still battling with my speech problem. Last year, I started speech therapy at the same time I began seeing Helene. Through the counseling process, I began to understand the roots of my problems. One of them was my extreme dependency on my mother. Ever since I was a child I had counted on her to tell me what to do; she was always there to pick up the pieces when I made the expected mistakes. I wasn't resentful, just scared that if I didn't listen I'd make the wrong decisions. And my insecurities continued to multiply as I failed in one pursuit after another. I was literally afraid to speak up for myself.

We took the therapy process step by step. And finally in one visualization, I was able to picture my mother—not hovering over me, but standing face to face. I looked her right in the eye and told her that it was time that she let me grow up and lead my own life, that I was ready to be responsible for myself.

That visualization really helped. Later, I was able to tell her the same thing in person. And since then, the two of us have really been getting along better and better.

With Helene's help, I also made peace with my father, and gave up some of the guilt I had been feeling since his death. I forgave him for the burdens he had placed on me as a child and he forgave me for hurting him.

According to Helene, my speech improved dramatically when I was relaxed in her office. Maybe that's true, but no matter how well people tell me I'm starting to talk, I still think I sound dumb. And that makes me feel dumb.

Sometimes, though, I surprise myself. Take the dental assistant program I decided to try last year despite my fears. I shocked myself by graduating second in my class. I even made a graduation speech and everyone understood and applauded. At about the same time, I also found the courage to begin speaking up in AA meetings.

Since my private therapy was helping so much, I decided to move on to group sessions. But that turned out to be a mistake. I couldn't handle a bunch of strangers listening to my pig-Latin.

So, true to my pattern, I quit working with Helene and also gave up on speech therapy. And because I felt so bad, I started gorging myself on fattening foods. I gained 30 pounds in just a few months. But at least I didn't go back to the bottle.

Fortunately, I didn't give up on myself entirely. There was still a part of me that was determined to survive.

Today, at 44 years old, I finally have a job that I enjoy. I'm a dental assistant. It's not public relations, but it's challenging and rewarding; I feel I'm really helping people. Meanwhile, my relationship with Arnold remains wonderful. Who would have believed that a man could have so much love and patience?

This time, I'm determined to stay on the wagon. Recently, I started speech therapy again, and I'm thinking about returning to counseling.

More than anything else in the world, I want my speech back. I'm convinced, you see, that if I could talk normally, there wouldn't be anything in the world that I couldn't do!

*　　*　　*　　*

Listen closely to Rose's last statement: "If I could talk normally, there wouldn't be anything in the world that I couldn't do." She's right and that petrifies her. The knowledge—and fear—that there's a whole world just waiting for her to make her mark may well have contributed to her speech problem ten years ago.

Since childhood, her insecurities have kept her from taking charge of her own life. And fear of the unknown continues to stifle her growth. She knows what life is like when she doesn't speak up, but she doesn't know what it would be like if she did.

When she first came to me, I could understand only about 50 percent of what she said. Then after just seven sessions, she was about 80 percent clear. I think she denies the progress because she's not yet ready to accept the success that her life is beginning to reflect.

When a mother constantly criticizes and directs her children, they lose confidence in themselves. Unfortunately, many parents make this mistake with the intention of protecting or teaching their children. In Rose's case, she decided early that she wasn't capable of making the right decisions, and so she learned not to trust herself. "After all, if Mom constantly criticizes me and makes my decisions for me, it must mean that I'm dumb, that I'm not capable of making decisions for myself."

Because she needed her mother's approval and acceptance in order to feel safe, she went out of her way to please her. "I'll do what you say, just love me."

Paradoxically, Rose also felt guilty for being her mother's favorite. Commonly, the family favorite feels, "I'm bad because I took all of Mom's attention." She may eventually feel the need to punish herself for this, as Rose might have done by picking an abusive husband and sabotaging her speech.

Rose felt stupid and her speech problem perpetuated the problem. People listening to her jumped to the conclusion that she was stupid. In this way, she got used to playing the victim. "I can't do it," she was saying, when, in truth, she wouldn't do it. She needed her physical impediment in order to say to her mother, "Look, Mom, I'm doing my best, but it's out of my control."

While Rose consciously attempted to please her mother, her subconscious anger festered inside. Although we often fall into the trap of trying to please others, we all resent people who won't let us

81

be ourselves. As I see it, *the parents' responsibility is not to run their children's life but merely to prepare them for it. The children's job, in turn, is to be who they uniquely are.*

Rose's mother was what I call a "parentaholic," someone who runs away from her own pain by focusing all her attention on her children. People who need to control others are usually terrified underneath. They feel, "If I don't control you, you won't love me because I'm worthless." Consider the times that you feel the need to control; it's usually when you're scared.

I would imagine that Rose's grandmother was the same way; because she wasn't satisfied with herself, she was probably critical of her daughter. Her daughter got the message that she wasn't enough, and she passed that feeling onto her own daughter. Thus, generation after generation perpetuates the mistake.

In this dependent kind of relationship, the child unconsciously feels she has to help her mother feel worthwhile, and so she doesn't have the opportunity to develop herself.

Unfortunately, when a child takes on the responsibility of making her mother feel good, she sets herself up to fail. She ends up feeling guilty for her parent's unhappiness. That's sad and destructive because no one can take the responsibility for anyone else's happiness; each of us is responsible for our own.

Initially, to help Rose get in touch with her feelings about her mother, I asked her to close her eyes and visualize their relationship. She pictured a very thick umbilical cord, which she felt both of them needed for their survival.

"I can't cut the cord," she told me, "because I need to nurture Mom and make her happy. I need to stay a child for her." When she said that, she noticed that her shoulders ached with the responsibility.

My job was to help her see that she was attempting an impossible task; that her mother's happiness was up to her mother alone. The only way Rose could help, I pointed out, was to feel better herself. Her mother would be happy just knowing that her daughter was doing better. To feel good, Rose had to learn to do what pleased her—not her mother.

But the little girl inside was still afraid that she couldn't survive without her mother. I told her to visualize her own adult part standing in front of the child, assuring her that *she* would take care of her.

Several sessions later, Rose again visualized the thick umbilical cord, but this time she was lugging a large machete. I encouraged her to cut the cord and say, "I am me and you are you. You don't need me for survival and I don't need you for survival."

We concluded that session with Rose adding, "Goodbye Mom,

hello Doris." She reinforced that experience with the affirmation, "I, Rose, am beginning to believe that I am capable of taking care of myself."

Generally, it's a good idea for older children, say by the time they turn 18, to start calling their parents by their first names. This helps them to see the adults as friends, rather than parents. And, in this way, they're able to start taking responsibility for themselves. As long as grown children continue to see their parents as "Mommy" and "Daddy," they will continue to see themselves as children. Each time they get together, they will inevitably fall into the old child-parent roles.

You've heard many parents say, "No matter what, you'll always be my child." Although they mean well, they're actually hurting their offspring. What I hear is, "I'll never let you grow up." If parents continue to treat their offspring as children, they will continue to act like children.

Try something. Close your eyes and see your Mom and Dad and call them by their first names; see them as people. If you can do this, you will be more accepting of them and less demanding. There comes a time when it's important to give up the old roles and become friends instead.

Perhaps you wouldn't choose your parents as friends. Well then, stop beating your head against the wall. We can love our parents without really liking them; and we don't have to feel guilty about it. If you're better off away from each other, then that's how it may need to be.

It's not worth making yourself sick over. But that's what we do; we make ourselves sick over all kinds of things that are difficult to face. I believe that most, if not all, disease is emotional in origin. The doctors, you recall, have never discovered a physical cause for Rose's speech impediment.

Besides the obvious psychosomatic illnesses, our mental state may also precipitate diseases like heart disease and even cancer. A person who is emotionally healthy usually experiences physical health as well. My theory is that our emotions affect our body chemistry and thus our immunity systems, the ability to fight sickness.

We know that stress and anger can cause high blood pressure and that extreme tension can cause ulcers. In this way, physical pain can be a symptom or warning that there's an emotional problem. People need to listen to their bodies, which are surprisingly literal.

As I have learned from my clients, for example, pain or illness in the ears may mean that the person does not want to hear; tension or problems in the eyes, that he does not want to see, and in the throat and tongue, that he does not want to speak. Often, a backache indicates anger; leg and stomach problems, fear; allergies, tension;

and blinding migraines, terror, rage and deep sadness that the victim doesn't want to see. After listening to their body, people have to learn to release their feelings in a healthy way. Some people get sick in order to rest; instead, they need to believe that it's okay to rest before they end up sick.

Rose slipped at work and broke her neck, the part of the body that separates the head from the heart. I don't believe this was a coincidence. By breaking her neck, Rose literally was cutting off her thoughts from her feelings. She was also acting out a part of her that wanted to die. Often, I find, alcoholics have a death wish. Alcohol is poison to them, and yet they keep taking it—killing themselves slowly but surely.

I don't believe it was a twist of fate either that robbed Rose of crisp, clear speech. Again, it was Rose herself who finally reached a point where she decided it was too scary to talk. Rather than continue to be abused by her husband, Rose stopped voicing her opinion, very nearly giving up speech entirely. I have no doubts that her speech impediment is emotional in origin, although her tongue muscles have probably grown lazy over the years. She was able to speak very clearly when she was relaxed in my office.

Obviously, Rose's speech impairment couldn't take the pain away. And so in order to drown that pain, she took up drinking.

Again, not mere chance. As a child, Rose felt responsible for her father's drinking problem. "If I were good enough, he wouldn't drink." And although Rose detested his drinking, she just naturally turned to the bottle for relief. (Remember, her father had a speech problem as well.)

We model ourselves after our parents, and from them, we learn our defenses. That's why it doesn't make sense to ask our children to "Do as I say, not as I do." It doesn't work that way.

Rose talks about "catching" her dad's alcoholism disease. She didn't actually catch it, but she did inherit the tendency. She followed his example of drinking and she ended up suffering from the same disease. I think that like the diabetic or the asthmatic, children inherit a physical weakness which predisposes them to certain conditions. Later, they may manifest the disease when their stress affects their weak point.

I'm excited about the progress Rose has made so far in her personal and professional life. Imagine making a speech in front of the whole graduating class! Although she has done her best to hide it, she is an extremely bright woman.

But even though she has finally found a man who gives her the love and respect she deserves, she isn't totally happy. Arnold can't give her happiness anymore than she could give it to her mother. *Happiness is a gift that only we can give to ourselves.*

Rose still has quite a bit of growing to do, and I hope she will continue. I'm convinced that when she stops sabotaging herself, she will be able to talk normally.

When she's ready to risk the unknown and accept the responsibility that goes along with speaking out, she'll be able to tell the world loudly and clearly what she thinks and feels.

Chapter 12 ──────────────────

Tom's Story:

I WON'T BE A SUCCESS BECAUSE THAT WOULD
PLEASE MOTHER AND I'M ANGRY AT HER

If success were measured by appearances, I had it all: A beautiful, intelligent wife, two good kids, two dogs, two Mercedes, a fancy address with a swimming pool, and a combined annual income of well over $100,000.

The sad part is that I was destroying everything I had, because I didn't feel successful. I was drinking too much, driving too fast, and playing too feverishly. My marriage was falling apart, and my sales career was moving in reverse.

Maybe if I'd been a doctor as I'd always wanted, I would have been happier and more successful in my career. I know it would have pleased my mother. Actually, I did manage to work my way through three years of pre-med before dropping out.

I took the easy road, a medical-equipment salesman instead of a doctor. And so I spent the next 25 years sitting on the edge of what I really wanted to do. In that time, my career was up and down so many times that I felt like I was on a seesaw.

I've always worked hard, and I couldn't understand why I wasn't moving up the ladder like everyone else. How I wanted the power I thought came with those promotions!

But I was never able to grasp it. And everytime the company clobbered me, I'd go home and kick the dogs, the kids and my wife. Or, worse, I wouldn't go home. For years I cheated on Lee. The irony is that instead of making me happy, it made things worse.

Ever since Lee and I were married, we've been tearing each other apart. Even on our honeymoon, I remember we argued about the value of public education. Lee is a public school administrator.

Although we've always loved each other, neither of us knew how to show that love. She would slice me in half with angry words and I would pretend not to care or even hear. The television was one of my biggest weapons; by turning on the set, I could turn off Lee and our problems. When I wasn't glued to the television, I was out flaunting my affairs. God knows how I managed to hurt the only woman I loved!

It was a schizoid life. At the same time we were battling each other, we were the classic parents, sacrificing ourselves for the children. For years we ignored our own needs and wants while we struggled to meet theirs. Lee and I went our separate ways except when we touched fingers with each other at Sunday dinner. It never occurred to me that by denying what was really upsetting me—the underlying feelings of dissatisfaction and unhappiness—I was destroying the family that was my primary reason for living.

When my family's very existence was threatened, my life caved in. The kids were off to college, things were horrendous at work, and Lee and I had separated. At 49 years old, I felt like I had fallen off the jungle gym. I was going through one helluva mid-life crisis.

My self-esteem had hit bottom, and without it, life wasn't worth a damn. I was scared, resentful and very angry. I was frustrated that no one at work took my ideas seriously, and I was jealous of Lee's career success.

At the same time, I was scared of losing her permanently. I felt so lonely. All I really wanted was for someone to hold me and love me. But I was too macho to ask. My knees were skinned and my pride bruised, and I felt powerless to do anything about it.

When I couldn't bear the pain any longer, I decided to go to Helene for therapy. But I wasn't too optimistic. I had walked out on a psychiatrist before because he called me "an emotional cripple."

This time was different. I can still remember the intensity of those first sessions. It's terrifying to tear down all the walls you've built to protect yourself. When you're done, there's nothing left for you to face but yourself.

I had lived with myself for half a century, and yet I didn't see the real me until I closed my eyes. All the unfinished business in my past had blinded me to who I really was and what I really wanted out of life.

As I became aware of my feelings through guided imagery, the whole picture began to take shape. What I saw behind all the pain and affairs, the power trips and the failures, was a scared little kid crying out for his mother's love.

For the first time, I understood that most of the fights with Lee were really fights with my mother. Even though I had moved across the country to get away from Mom, I had brought the problems with me. Instead of resolving them, I merely turned my anger and hurt on the new woman in my life.

I had spent a lifetime trying to win my mother's love and

approval, but no matter what I did, it wasn't enough. Mother criticized me for everything. I was convinced that I wasn't as smart or as good or as thoughtful as my brothers and sisters. So early on, I made the decision that I wasn't okay, that I'd never be enough.

By the time I was an adult, I was driven by my craving for my mother's affection. I even tried to buy it, sending her every bit of money I could spare. "Here, Mother, is everything I have. Now, will you love me?"

To be fair, I know she didn't have it easy. My Dad died when I was 14, and mother rotated through five more marriages. She was a dumpy, little frumpy lady, but she must have had some kind of sex appeal. She was remarkable in many ways and I loved her very much. For me, she became the symbol of the love I'd always needed and couldn't get from women.

One day in therapy, I visualized her standing in front of me, and I was a little child. All the unconscious pain poured out of me. "I hate you," I yelled. "All you ever did was criticize me. I did everything I could to be a good son to you, but it was never enough. I gave you all I had, but you wanted more. I'm angry at you and I'll show you. I'll never be a doctor like you want me to be; I'll never succeed at any career!"

I imagined that a little pillow I was holding in my arms was my mother, and right there on the mattress I started choking her. "You made me feel unlovable; you made me feel weak and useless," I yelled. "You took away all my personal power." I squeezed the pillow until the image of my mother went limp in my hands.

I was free of her at last, and I felt relieved. Twelve years after my mother had actually died, I killed her in my visualization. And only then was I free of her negative effect on me.

I began to realize that I'd been transferring my feelings towards my mother to my wife and even my boss. Because I felt Mother had hurt me, I was afraid to let anybody close to me. So while I sought recognition through my lovers and bosses, I pushed away the very people who could give it to me.

In my favorite visualization, I climbed to the top of a mountain. At the summit, I received the gift of wisdom and love from a whole world of people. They enjoyed me for who I was and what I was. On the mountaintop, I gave and received love freely. And I started to reclaim my personal power.

I began to understand the futility of my long struggle for control over other people. I took a close look at those in charge of my company and I saw that frequently the ones at the top are the ones who stab the most and stab the best. I didn't need or want that shallow, cruel kind of power.

What I'd really been missing was the inner power that I'd given

89

up to my mother. Other people don't stop us, I discovered, we stop ourselves. When I understood that, I no longer felt the need to claw my way to the top.

As soon as I was willing to give up that type of power, I found my own, the kind that no one else can take away from me. From that day on, I re-owned my peaceful, inner strength.

Whenever I need to feel safe and strong, I return to that mountaintop. Up there, my success and happiness seem well within my reach.

I've come to understand that my job as a medical-equipment salesman isn't what I want. I'm a people person; I have a tremendous need to reach out to others. So, since I was so excited about my own success in therapy, I decided to go back to college to get a masters degree in psychology. I've just completed the work and I hope to start my own practice as soon as I pass the state exam. I feel good about my career goals for the first time in my life.

And for the first time in almost 30 years, I'm happy being monogamous. In addition to loving Lee, I've come to admire and enjoy her strengths. She also went through the therapy process and has grown along with me. It turns out that I wasn't the only one competing for the upper hand in that marriage. While I was fighting my mother, Lee was waging a similar battle with her brother.

With the wars behind us, we're free now to accept each other, warts and all. Last year, Helene remarried us symbolically in her office, and we're happier than either of us thought possible. I saved a copy of our new marriage vows, and I re-read them when I need a reminder:

"I am a human being, just like you.
I have feelings.
At times, I feel happiness, joy or excitement.
At other times, I feel sad, angry or scared.
I want to communicate all my feelings to you.
And I want to feel good when I am with you,
As well as when we are apart.
I enjoy sharing time with you
And I need to know that I am a whole person by myself.
I want to be loved unconditionally,
Respected, trusted and appreciated.
I am a human being, just like you."

At this point in my life, I feel I finally know the real meaning of personal success and power. It's certainly not striking out at other people or even controlling them. It's finding a delightful way to fulfill myself. It's being able to start my day with enthusiasm and end it with a high. It's an inner feeling of contentment that feels like an orgasm of the soul.

*   *   *   *

Those certainly don't sound like the words of an "emotional cripple." Fear can inhibit anyone of us, but problems like Tom's are not incurable. By providing the tools to face that fear and deal with it, therapy helped Tom walk again in just four months. And this time he's walking in the direction *he* wants to go.

I'm proud of both Tom and Lee's progress. They had damaged their relationship severely by the time they asked for help. Their anger was intense, and their fears deep.

As sad as it was, their situation wasn't much different from many of ours. One cause for so many unsuccessful marriages is our lack of social education. No one teaches us the necessary communication skills or shows us how to build our self-esteem, which are both vital to a successful relationship.

I see every relationship as composed of three parts. Picture a bridge: The two partners form the foundation, and the communication forms the actual bridge. Obviously, the foundation must be strong or the bridge will collapse.

A good foundation is built upon strong self-esteem. Tom and Lee's self-esteem was low, and so their foundation was weak. To strengthen it, they had to feel good about themselves, eliminate their negative decisions and replace them with positive ones.

Their communication was also poor. To make their bridge more stable, they had to learn how to interact with each other, to tell each other the truth about their feelings.

I worked with Tom and Lee in separate sessions to strengthen their self-esteem (the foundation) and in combined sessions to improve their communication (their bridge).

In the process, we discovered that jealousy was creating a big rift in their relationship. Tom was jealous of Lee's career success, and Lee was jealous of Tom's affairs with other women.

In my opinion, jealousy is only a symptom. The real cause is a feeling of not being enough. When Tom cheated on Lee, he pushed a button on her internal tape recorder that said, "See, you are not enough." By doing so well in her career, Lee unwittingly pushed a similar button on Tom's tape recorder. Both of them were replaying tapes that they originally made when they were young children.

And both of them were too proud to tell the other how they really felt. Tom was too scared to tell Lee that he was hurting.

When they first came to me, Tom sat calmly smiling, with his hands clasped behind his head. Lee was furious at him for what she perceived as his indifference. And the angrier she got, the more he pretended to be unaffected. At the same time that Tom said he wanted to reunite with his wife, his prideful behavior was pushing her further away. False pride was keeping them apart.

Pride is a disguise or protection. With pride, we try to cover up our real feelings of vulnerability, fear and hurt. Underneath the pride, we're saying, "I won't let you know how much you can hurt me. I won't let you know that I need you, your help and your love"

False pride is the easy way out, but it doesn't get you what you want. It takes courage to tell someone your true feelings, but it's worth the effort. Sharing your true self with someone you love can bring you much closer together.

In separate sessions, I asked Tom and Lee what they wanted to do about their negative feelings for each other. Not surprisingly, they admitted that they were angry enough to kill each other. So there in the safety of my office, they yelled and screamed, beat on a mattress and strangled pillows. When they had vented all the rage, they realized that they still loved each other very much.

I have found that I never have to help anyone love another person. I just have to help them release the anger that's blocking their love feelings.

Love is a deep feeling that can't be created or denied. You can't *stop* loving, so it's useless to try. Those who believe they have stopped loving are usually just blocking their love feelings.

Hate can block love. Sometimes, it damages that love beyond repair, and divorce is the best solution. But, more often than not, couples rediscover their love as soon as they're able to release their pain and resentment.

Once Tom and Lee worked on rebuilding their own self-esteem, they were able to show their love and finally to accept each other's.

Like most of us, Lee and Tom had brought to their marriage their excess baggage from childhood, and it was weighing down their lives together. For protection, even from each other, they had built fortresses around themselves. They ended up safe, but lonely and miserable.

Tom's wall, as he discovered in a visualization, was nine feet high and made of concrete. One problem was that it couldn't protect him from himself. Angry at his mother, he had spent his life rebelling. To spite her, he took a job he didn't really want. And because he didn't like what he was doing, he never succeeded at it. By sabotaging his success, he perpetuated his low self-esteem. He felt powerless, and yet he was looking for power in all the wrong places.

One way he took control and felt powerful was through his passive aggressive behavior. Passive aggression is a defense, which usually isn't premeditated or deliberately malicious. It comes in many forms; among them, sarcasm, withdrawal, procrastination, tardiness, and forgetfulness. Showing up late or forgetting an important date are ways a passive aggressor gets back or expresses resentment towards others. As a result, the other person is likely to end up feeling unimportant. (Note: Such actions don't always indicate passive aggression; they may mean only that this person's values are different from yours.)

In its extreme, the passive aggressive pattern can be a serious threat to the individual as well as society. The meek person who suffers for years in silence is like a time bomb. When he finally lets his anger loose, he can explode, literally killing anyone in his path. Fortunately, Tom took care of those feelings in my office, where no one was hurt.

The passive aggressor is the one who has the control in a relationship. When Lee was angry and yelled at him, Tom saw not only her rage but his mother's as well. And that scared him, increasing his feeling of powerlessness. So he withdrew, refusing to fight. That gave him the edge, because the worst thing we can do to another person is to ignore them. It's like telling them that they don't exist, and that's terrifying. Tom did that to Lee by turning on the television, pretending he didn't care, and running around with other women.

To get back at his wife (and his mother) for hurting his feelings and making him feel powerless, he hit Lee where it hurt the most. He collected women like some men collect coins. But each affair was only a temporary high; the good feelings never lasted, because they came from outside.

In one therapy session, I asked Tom to picture himself stepping inside his penis. He imagined becoming his penis and watched himself moving towards a chorus line of vaginas. "I'll show you my power," the penis threatened.

From this experience, Tom could see that he was being sexual with women in order to feel this power. The need to feel powerful over someone else means that we feel powerless inside. "Go back to the first time you felt powerless," I suggested to Tom.

He was a young child back home with his mother. "What do you want to tell her? What do you want to do to her?"

Tom has told you the rest. He wanted to kill his mother, and so he did in his visualization.

He had felt powerless with his mother, and he transferred that feeling to the other women in his life. Promiscuity was one way he was trying to take back his power. Tom was also saying, "I'll give you my penis, but not the rest of me."

When he was finally able to free himself from his mother's

93

control, he could reclaim his own power. In his visualization, he watched it leave his penis and travel up to his heart. He was finally able to see that his real power is love.

True power is feeling good about yourself—liking and loving yourself. It's knowing that you are okay, competent and lovable, even though you make mistakes. Power is having the confidence to do what you want to do. If you're really powerful, you don't have to prove it to yourself or others. You just feel it.

Look at some of the executives in your own company. Are they powerful or merely power-hungry? So many people believe that if they move up the ladder, they will feel powerful. But it seldom happens. Instead, every rung of the ladder brings with it another disappointment. And they continue driving themselves upward no matter what and who they hurt.

I believe there are many unhappy executives still fighting their moms or dads or brother or sisters for the upper hand. Too often, they use their "powerful" positions to put down others and blame them for their own mistakes and shortcomings. They constantly have to prove their strength, because they really don't *feel* it inside.

An insecure executive builds his strength by trying to weaken others; an executive who feels powerful inside can delegate authority without being afraid to lose it himself. He is comfortable in his belief that he can be powerful, and so can others. The person who has the clean, pure power at the top is the one who is satisfied that he is fulfilling his own potential and wants to help others do the same.

Tom is well on his way to feeling that kind of power. After punishing himself for half his life with a job he didn't want to do, he's finally able to move on. Psychology seems the perfect choice of careers. Tom is a tremendously caring, nurturing person with a need to give. He has always wanted to be a healer, and now that he has healed himself, he is ready to help others.

PART III
The Tools

Chapter 13 —————————————————

Close Your Eyes
And See Clearly

Power is the key to happiness and success. Not the external kind of power that goes with the key to the executive washroom or the gold wedding band, but the internal power that allows us to build the life we want for ourselves.

All of us are carpenters. In order to become masters, we need some basic theory and the proper tools.

The following principles are the foundation upon which we can begin to build our lives to our specifications in order to create success:

1. Every human being is basically good.

2. We naturally make the right decisions unless taught otherwise.

3. We all need love and acceptance in order to grow.

4. One way we learn is by modeling ourselves after others, particularly our parents.

5. In order to become a whole person and to experience inner peace, we need to re-own and balance our four parts: Physical, emotional, intellectual and spiritual.

6. We are not able to live in the present until we finish unfinished business from the past.

7. It is human to feel scared at times, and if we don't acknowledge our fears, we tend to behave either

aggressively by attacking others, or passively by withdrawing.

8. We need to experience and accept all our feelings, including fear and anger, before we can truly accept ourselves and others.

9. Then we have to release our negative feelings in a safe, constructive way so that we can make room for new positive feelings.

10. Since we make decisions based on our experiences, we need to create new positive experiences.

In the building or growth process, we first need to get in touch with one of our fundamental negative beliefs. Then, we must go back to the time we originally made that decision, re-experience our painful feelings and release them in a safe way. For example, if we're angry, we can hit a pillow and yell at an image of the person we're upset with. Then, after we have released the feelings, we can create a new positive experience by visualizing the scene just the way we wanted it to be. That way we experience positive feelings and can make new, positive decisions. Finally, we have to reinforce the new decisions with affirmations and continue to visualize what we want in our lives.

Visualization is nothing new; we visualize all the time. Imagery is the language of the unconscious. Dreams, for example, are our subconscious talking to us. Through guided imagery exercises, we bridge the conscious with the unconscious so that we can understand how our feelings and thoughts are affecting our actions.

When we hurt, we waste our precious time trying to guard ourselves against our pain. The alcoholic drowns his pain; the foodaholic stuffs it, the workaholic runs away from it, and the thinkaholic tries to reason it away.

By learning to face and understand our feelings, we're able to release the destructive ones in a safe way. When we no longer need to run away from or defend ourselves against fear, anger and hurt, we have no use for our crutches, like food, alcohol and work. That's when we start to succeed.

The following exercises will help you conquer your Fear of Success by helping you get in touch with the roots of your unhappiness. Then, they will provide you with the tools that you need to break through and make new roots so that you can attain success.

Read through each exercise completely before beginning. Until you become familiar with them, you may want to limit yourself to one at a time. If you have trouble remembering the whole visuali-zation, you can ask someone to read it to you. It's very important that you feel comfortable with this person. If you feel silly or self-conscious, you may want to put the exercises on tape and work by yourself. If you do, make sure that you pause frequently to give yourself time to complete each step.

YOUR SAFE PLACE

Everyone needs a place where they feel safe. When you're work-ing with your Fears of Success, it's especially important to feel secure and protected. It doesn't really matter whether the place you choose is real or imaginery.

Do this exercise every time you begin working in guided im-agery. Find a comfortable place to sit or lie down. Make sure it's someplace where you won't be disturbed or distracted. Surround yourself with several soft pillows.

Close your eyes and take two deep breaths. Check your body for tension. If you feel tense anywhere, tell that part to relax. Take two deep breaths and see clean, fresh air flowing into the area to bring it deeper relaxation.

Imagine a place where you'd like to be right now, a place where you feel safe and at peace. It could be a beach, forest, meadow, mountaintop or cloud. Or it could be your own bedroom or back-yard. You are limited only by your own imagination. Do what you want in order to feel safer. For example, if you need extra protec-tion, you might want to build a wall or a house or imagine white light around you.

What are you seeing? What are you hearing? How are you feel-ing?

This paradise that you have created is yours alone; it will be waiting for you whenever you need it. Whenever you feel frightened or unhappy, you can return to it and feel safe again.

When you're ready to leave, take two more complete breaths and open your eyes.

MEET YOUR WISE PERSON

We all have a part of us that is very knowledgeable and wise. This is called our high conscious, spiritual or intuitive part. It is not affected by society's teachings or our own fears. We can reach this part by getting in touch with our wise person. Sometimes, the wise person is God, a light, a color, father time, a wise Indian, a fairy godmother, someone we love and respect, or even ourselves. When our conscious mind doesn't know the answer to something, we can always call on our wise person.

In this exercise, I'd like you to meet your wise person and become comfortable with him, her or it. Close your eyes, relax and return to your safe place. Allow yourself to see your wise person, who is all good and knowing. Your wise person is bathed in white light and is coming towards you now, getting closer and closer. The image is getting much clearer. What does he or she look like?

Do you trust your wise person? If not, let the image go and make room for another wise person to come to you. It must be someone that you trust to give you the answers you're seeking.

Say hello to your image and share your feelings. Tell your wise person that you will be back later to talk some more, that you are glad you found him or her. Take two deep breaths and open your eyes.

TALK WITH YOUR WISE PERSON

It's important to remember that your wise person is a part of you. In this exercise, you will have the opportunity to talk with that part, which will answer all your questions.

So first take a few deep breaths, relax and go to your safe place. Allow your wise person to come towards you. See the image standing in front of you. Ask him or her anything you want about success. Why are you unhappy or unfulfilled? What do you need to do in order to move on?

Now, imagine that you are the wise person. Step into his body, put on his shoes and dress yourself in his clothes. Then, see an image of yourself standing in front of you. And as the wise person, answer your question.

Continue to ask your wise person any questions you have. With each answer, step into your wise person's body, see an image of yourself in front of you, and answer the question.

After you've listened to all the answers, your wise person will give you a gift to help you. Allow yourself to receive the gift and see what it is.

If you don't understand what the gift means, then become the wise person and explain it. If you wish, thank him for the gift.

Remember that you can always call on your wise person when you need answers, guidance or protection.

Take two deep breaths and slowly open your eyes.

LISTEN TO YOUR BODY

When you check your body out for tension, what do you feel? Does your head hurt? Do you feel tightness in your back and shoulders? Do your legs or stomach ache?

I have discovered that suppressed emotions can cause physical pain and even illness. Aches and pains are your body's way of talking to you.

Fear, I have found, is usually indicated by tension or pain in the stomach, thighs, legs or feet. Anger festers in the back, forehead, arms, hands, jaws, teeth and center of the back of the neck. Sadness lies in the sinuses, sides of the back of the neck and center of the chest.

Your body is more literal than you might think. Tension in specific areas often means:

Chest—"I feel stifled or suffocated."
Eyes—"I don't want to see_____."
Ears—"I don't want to hear_____."
Hands—"I don't know what to do" or "I cannot handle it."
Knees—"I can't stand on my own two feet."
Throat—"I am afraid to say_____."
Heart—"I have a broken heart."

A man who suffers from impotency or a woman who is not sexually responsive may be feeling, "I don't want to be vulnerable, so I am closing down" or "I am afraid of my own sexuality" or "I'm angry or hurt and so I won't let him/her in."

And someone who complains that he is "falling apart at the seams" may literally end up suffering from arthritis.

It's my theory that even teenage acne may result from tension that constricts the blood vessels, thus cutting down circulation and leaving the body more prone to infection. I don't believe it's a co-incidence that the teenager who is so tense and concerned about his or her appearance ends up with blemishes all over the face.

To get in touch with the language of your body, close your eyes and take two deep breaths. Check your body out for tension from your toes to the top of your head.

Find the tension and identify your feelings, whether they be fear, anger or sadness. Express your feelings in words or by direct action. For example, if you feel angry, yell, "I am angry!" Make a fist and beat a soft pillow.

Be aware of who is triggering your anger, and imagine that he or she is standing in front of you now. Remember, that person can even be yourself. Tell him how you feel. Explain why you are feeling angry, and what you want him to do or stop doing.

Continue with this exercise until there is no more tension in your body. When your body feels relaxed, take two deep breaths and slowly open your eyes.

Chapter 14 ————————————

You Can Have It All

Negative thoughts keep us stuck in one place. So in order to move on in your life, it's necessary to substitute positive thoughts for the negative ones. These are called affirmations.

I recommend that you end each of your guided imagery exercises with an affirmation. Before we go any further in the visualization process, then, let's discuss how to make them.

With a little determination, you can turn any negative thought into a positive one. Listen to your daily thoughts and conversations. Whenever you hear a negative thought, change it to a positive one. After awhile, you will begin to do it automatically.

Some negative thoughts are harder to erase than others. Make a list of yours on a piece of paper. Write at the top, "I am afraid that _____" and fill in the blank with whatever negative thoughts come to mind.

Pick out one, and change it to a positive thought. Start with the word, "I," followed by your name and the new thought.

For example: The negative thought or fear may be, "I am afraid that I don't deserve money." The affirmation changes this to, "I, Your Name, do deserve money."

Repeat or write your affirmations several times and/or put them on tape and play them back. Repetition is important, so review them often.

Now, substitute "You" and "She" for "I." For example, "You, Your Name, do deserve money." And, "She, Your Name, does deserve money."

Don't panic if you don't believe your affirmation right away. Give it a few weeks of repetition to sink in.

If you're still uncomfortable with it, try watering it down a little: "I, Your Name, am beginning to believe that I deserve some money." We are capable of moving on only when we're able to accept ourselves and to feel comfortable with where we are at the moment.

If you still don't believe the new affirmation, then write your negative thought on a piece of paper. Follow it by the word "because" and list the reasons.

For example, "I, Your Name, don't deserve some money because:

1. I stole a dollar from my father when I was a child.
2. I don't know how to handle money.
3. I'm afraid it will make me greedy for more.
4. I'm worthless.

Now, take one reason at a time and change it with an affirmation:

Number 1 becomes, "I, Your Name, forgive myself for taking a dollar from my father when I was a child."

Number 2 becomes, "I, Your Name, am beginning to believe that I know how to handle money."

Number 3 becomes, "I, Your Name, believe that I can have money and be generous."

Number 4 becomes, "I, Your Name, am a worthwhile person."

If you're still not convinced, you have more work to do. Write your affirmation on the left hand side of a piece of paper, and your feelings on the right. Continue to do this until you are finally ready to accept your affirmation. For example:

I, Your Name, deserve money.	No, I don't.
I, Your Name, deserve money.	No way.
I, Your Name, deserve money.	Why?
I, Your Name, deserve money.	Why not?
I, Your Name, deserve money.	Well, maybe.
I, Your Name, deserve money.	Well, maybe a little.
I, Your Name, deserve money.	Yes, I do deserve money.

If this doesn't help, and you find yourself getting increasingly more negative, you probably have to dig a little deeper. Perhaps there is another negative thought underneath the one you've been working on. For example, behind "I don't deserve money," could be "Money is evil."

Now, start the affirmation process again from the beginning with the new negative thought. If you weren't able to find another negative thought, ask yourself what you're getting out of holding onto the original, "I don't deserve money." Chances are that you're staying safe.

Here are several more suggestions when working with affirmations:

• Keep them short.
• Use only positive words. Instead of, "I am not bad," say,

"I am good."

- Stay in the present. Avoid statements like, "I will" or "I hope to." Instead, say, "I am."
- Work on only a few affirmations at a time.

To help you get started, I have made a long list of affirmations. After you get used to using them, you may want to substitute others that more closely apply to your individual situation. Remember each time to fill in your own name after the "I".

Here are some suggested affirmations that you can begin working with in all seven areas of Fear of Success:

FEAR OF THE UNKNOWN

1. I, Your Name, am experiencing new things (a job, relationship, vacation) even though they are scary and unfamiliar.
2. I, _____, am beginning to believe that I have the courage to face the unknown.
3. I, _____, want to be satisfied in my life so I am willing to take risks.
4. I, _____, am taking risks in order to get what I want, even though I am scared.
5. I, _____, am scared and I have the courage to do what I want.
6. I, _____, want to say when I retire that I did what I wanted to do.
7. I, _____, want to be able to say on my dying bed that I really lived.
8. I, _____, am truly alive when I'm doing what I want to do.
9. I, _____, am ready to face the unknown, even though it is scary.
10. I, _____, am visualizing the way I want my job and/or relationship to be, and I am allowing myself to move on.

FEAR THAT SUCCESS DOES NOT FIT MY IMAGE OF MYSELF

1. I, _____, am seeing a positive image of myself.
2. I, _____, am seeing myself with an abundance of love.
3. I, _____, am seeing myself with an abundance of prosperity.
4. I, _____, am seeing myself successful.
5. I, _____, am seeing myself happy and healthy.
6. I, _____, am seeing myself thin.
7. I, _____, am seeing myself as a manager.
8. I, _____, am seeing myself in a fulfilling relationship.
9. I, _____, am seeing myself in clothes that reflect my success.
10. I, _____, accept my new, successful image of myself.

FEAR THAT I DON'T DESERVE SUCCESS
1. I, _____, am beginning to believe that I might deserve to be happy and successful.
2. I, _____, am beginning to believe that I deserve to have what I want in my life.
3. I, _____, accept that I've always done the best I could.
4. I, _____, accept that I'm human and it's okay for me to make mistakes.
5. I, _____, am learning from my mistakes.
6. I, _____, forgive myself for all my mistakes.
7. I, _____, am letting go of my guilt feelings and allowing myself to be successful and happy.
8. I, _____, believe that it is my birthright to be happy and successful.
9. I, _____, deserve success in my relationships and in my career.
10. I, _____, deserve to have it all.

FEAR THAT PEOPLE WILL NOT LIKE ME IF I'M SUCCESSFUL
1. I, _____, am successful and people are happy for me.
2. I, _____, am successful and I have many friends.
3. I, _____, am meeting people who support my successes.
4. I, _____, am modeling success and happiness for my friends.
5. I, _____, am successful in my career and people want to be with me.
6. I, _____, am successful in my career and I am in a fulfilling relationship.
7. I, _____, am happy and other people who want to feel good are attracted to me.
8. I, _____, am wealthy and I have many friends.
9. I, _____, am a top executive and I have many caring people in my life.
10. I, _____, am slim and attractive and my peers appreciate me.

FEAR THAT SUCCESS HAS SOME SCARY CONSEQUENCES
1. I, _____, am wealthy and I am a good, caring person.
2. I, _____, am rich and happy.
3. I, _____, am prosperous and honest.
4. I, _____, use money as a tool to help me create what I want for myself and others.
5. I, _____, believe there is an abundance of money in this world.
6. I, _____, am wealthy and people want to be with me because I am me.
7. I, _____, am successful and I have enough time for myself and

my family.
8. I, _____, am successful and I balance my life between work and play.
9. I, _____, am in a loving relationship and I am free to be me.
10. I, _____, am in a fulfilling relationship and I am sharing the responsibilities with my partner.
11. I, _____, believe I am able to change my commitments to others.
12. I, _____, am in a relationship and I keep my power to be me, to say and do what I really want.
13. I, _____, am in a lasting, loving relationship.
14. I, _____, accept that there is an abundance of food in my life.
15. I, _____, am slim and strong.
16. I, _____, am slim and safe.
17. I, _____, am attractive and I can handle all the I attention I get.
18. I, _____, am attractive and other people appreciate my personality and intelligence as well as my looks.
19. I, _____, can say no and I am okay.
20. I, _____, have it all and I am safe.

FEAR THAT MY PARENTS WON'T LOVE ME IF I'M MORE SUCCESSFUL THAN THEY

1. I, _____, am successful and my parents love me.
2. I, _____, believe that my parents want me to be as happy and as successful as I can be.
3. I, _____, please my parents when I am happy and use all my potential.
4. I, _____, accept that I can be happier and more successful than my parents because opportunities are so much better now.
5. I, _____, am earning much more money than my father and he is very pleased and proud of me.

FEAR THAT TO BE SUCCESSFUL IS TO FULFILL MY PARENTS' AMBITIONS

1. I, _____, am successful because I want to be.
2. I, _____, accept that my parents did the best they could.
3. I, _____, accept that my parents are human beings with feelings and insecurities just like mine.
4. I, _____, forgive my parents for all their mistakes.
5. I, _____, love and accept my parents.

GENERAL FEAR OF SUCCESS

1. I, _____, am a worthwhile person.

2. I, _____, am important.
3. I, _____, am lovable.
4. I, _____, am special.
5. I, _____, am enough.
6. I, _____, am attractive.
7. I, _____, have a nice body.
8. I, _____, am healthy.
9. I, _____, am creative.
10. I, _____, am intelligent.
11. I, _____, am responsible.
12. I, _____, am trustworthy.
13. I, _____, am efficient.
14. I, _____ am organized.
15. I, _____, am competent.
16, I, _____, am talented.
17. I, _____, am a good athlete.
18. I, _____, have a beautiful singing voice.
19. I, _____, am a good musician.
20. I, _____, am honest.
21. I, _____, am good-looking.
22. I, _____, have a good mind and body.
23. I, _____, am a good person.
24. I, _____, am a caring person.
25. I, _____, am a considerate person.
26. I, _____, have many friends.
27. I, _____, feel I belong.
28. I, _____, am feeling my inner power.
29. I, _____, am owning my power and I am directing it in a positive way.
30. I, _____, have an abundance of male and female friends.
31. I, _____, am accepting the importance of playing.
32. I, _____, accept that play rejuvenates me and helps me work more efficiently.
33. I, _____, am balancing my four parts: Mental, physical, emotional and spiritual.
34. I, _____, am a whole person.
35. I, _____, trust myself to know who to trust.
36. I, _____, trust my intuition.
37. I, _____, accept all my feelings and express them in a constructive way.
38. I, _____, am accepting that it is okay for me to be scared or angry.
39. I, _____, can express my anger in a safe way.
40. I, _____, can control my anger.
41. I, _____, can be angry and I'm still a lady/gentleman.

42. I, _____, am expressing my anger at a pillow and I am safe and so are others.
43. I, _____, have everything inside of me to make me happy.
44. I, _____, am taking time to hear what my scared child is afraid of and I'm comforting and reassuring him/her.
45. I, _____, am willing to acknowledge that I have fears and I have the courage to express them to people I trust.
46. I, _____, am in control of what food or liquid I put into my body.
47. I, _____, only put things into my body that help keep me healthy and attractive.
48. I, _____, understand the importance of taking care of my body.
49. I, _____, take care of my body and my body takes care of me.
50. I, _____, accept that I always do the best I can at the time.
51. I, _____, accept that I have choices in my life.
52. I, _____, am looking at my choices.
53. I, _____, trust my ability to choose what is right for me.
54. I, _____, am learning from my past and letting go of it so that I can live in the present.
55. I, _____, am focusing on what I can do right now because that is all I'm in control of.
56. I, _____, am ready to re-own my birthright to be me.
57. I, _____, am free to be me.
58. I, _____, am exploring who I really am.
59. I, _____, am free to re-own and experience my sexual feelings in a healthy way.
60. I, _____, accept that my sexual desires are normal, healthy feelings and I can choose when to act on them.
61. I, _____, am telling my partner what I want sexually.
62. I, _____, am communicating honestly and clearly.
63. I, _____, am really listening to what others have to say.
64. I, _____, am being my unique self because it feels good and that's my gift to the world.
65. I, _____, understand that when I am self-caring, I can be there for others.
66. I, _____, like myself.
67. I, _____, love myself unconditionally.
68. I, _____, am creating that perfect job for me.
69. I, _____, am finding the best place for me to live.
70. I, _____, am allowing my perfect mate to come into my life.
71. I, _____, am meeting my best friend.
72. I, _____, am meeting a soulmate.
73. I, _____, have an abundance of love in my life.
74. I, _____, am allowing prosperity into my life.
75. I, _____, am allowing money to flow to me effortlessly and in

a healthy way.

76. I, _____, accept that I did my best as a parent.
77. I, _____, forgive myself for any hurts I may have caused my children.
78. I, _____, am letting go of my children and allowing them to be responsible for their own lives.
79. I, _____, am only responsible for my own actions and feelings.
80. I, _____, am creating what I want in my life.

Now that you understand how to make affirmations, you can move on to more exercises that can help you recognize and conquer your Fears of Success.

Chapter 15 _____

Close Your Eyes
And See More Clearly

To get in touch with your Fears of Success, you have to connect with the unconscious feelings that have been running your life.

Imagine a house that's uncomfortably cold because the heating isn't working. To repair the system so that everything works to its full capacity, you have to go down to the basement to fix the furnace.

It's the same for people. When your life isn't working out the way you want it to, you have to "go down to the furnace" to uncover the unconscious negative thoughts that are keeping you from reaching your full potential. The following exercises include the rest of the tools you need to recognize and overcome the blocks to your success.

EXERCISE 1: MESSAGE ABOUT SUCCESS

Negative messages about success can block you and keep you from getting what you want. So, your job is to find out what those negative messages are and then replace them with positive ones.

Close your eyes and relax. Take two complete breaths. Imagine that you're flying through the sky. Dip your wings and turn to the left. You're flying back to a time in your childhood when you received or made a negative decision about success.

Look down and see that time. Allow yourself to land. Where are you? About how old are you? What's happening? What are you thinking? How are you feeling?

Are you ready to change that message? If you are, then imagine yourself changing it. Create a new scene in which you are making or receiving a positive message.

Now, what are you thinking? How are you feeling?

Imagine that you are telling someone your new decision about success, and that they are very happy for you.

Take two big breaths and open your eyes. To reinforce your new positive message, make an affirmation. For example: Old message, "Let the boys win in sports or they won't want to play with you." Affirm, "I, Your Name, am winning and men like to play with me." Old message, "Artists starve." Affirm, "I, Your Name, am making a good living as an artist."

EXERCISE 2: BELIEVING THAT YOU DESERVE SUCCESS

We're going to work here on letting go of your negative feelings about yourself, so that you can believe that you deserve happiness and success.

Close your eyes, relax and take two deep breaths.

See a bag of garbage in front of you. It's stuffed with scraps of paper listing all the bad feelings you have about yourself and others.

It took you years to collect all this garbage. You picked up some from people who told you by their words or behavior that you weren't okay. The rest came from your own guilt feelings or decisions that you're bad or not enough.

How big is your bag of garbage? How heavy is it?

Where in your body are you carrying it? Is it in your stomach or back, your shoulders or someplace else?

Now, open this bag and look at the contents.

Are you ready to start getting rid of this excess baggage? Are you willing to give it up so that you can be free to move on in your life?

If you are, then open your garbage bag. Pick out one piece of paper that contains a negative thought or feeling that you're ready to let go of.

Go back to the time when you were given that negative message. Be there now.

Where are you? About how old are you? Who's with you? What is he/she saying?

Watch and experience yourself accepting the garbage that he's dealing out. How are you feeling? What do you think you're getting out of accepting this junk?

You don't need it; hand it back. Tell the other person, "This is your garbage. I don't need it anymore. I am okay."

See him taking back the garbage; after all, it's his stuff. How do you feel?

And now imagine that you are writing a new positive thought with a colorful pen on a big piece of paper.

Take two breaths and open your eyes. Actually write down your affirmation and put it up someplace where you will see it often,

110

like the bathroom mirror, closet or refrigerator door. For example: Garbage, "You deserve to be punished because you broke your wedding vows." Affirm, "I, Your Name, am okay and I deserve to be happy in another marriage."

EXERCISE 3: BURN THE REST OF THE GARBAGE

If you still have more garbage, you may want to get rid of it by burning it.

Close your eyes, take two deep breaths and relax. Visualize your bag of garbage again. Imagine that you're standing with your bag in front of a large fireplace with a roaring fire.

Take out a single piece of paper with a bad feeling or thought about yourself or others written on it. See the words clearly.

How do you feel? Are you ready to let go of that piece of trash? If you are, crumple it up now and throw it into the flames. Watch how quickly it burns.

Imagine that you're writing a new positive thought or feeling on a piece of posterboard with a bright-colored magic marker.

How do you feel? Take two deep breaths and open your eyes. Write down your new, positive thought, or affirmation, and put it someplace where you can see it often.

Remember that whenever you wish, you can return to the fireplace and burn another piece of garbage or give it back to whomever gave it to you in the first place. Each time you do so, you'll be making room for more positive thoughts and feelings.

EXERCISE 4: CONFRONTING A FEAR AND CUTTING THE ROPE

This exercise will help you get in touch with one fear you have about success and break through it.

Close your eyes, relax and take two complete breaths.

See yourself successful in whatever area you choose. Watch yourself getting what you want or being who you want to be. Now tune into your fear by saying, "I am afraid that _____." Complete the sentence.

Go back to the time when you first experienced that fear. Be there now. If you need protection, ask your wise person to be there with you.

Where are you? About how old are you? What's happening? What are you thinking? What negative decision are you making about yourself, other people or life in general? How are you feeling?

Tell the person or persons with you how you're feeling. Remember, you're safe; there are no consequences to what you say. If

111

you're concerned about the noise, place a pillow over your mouth.

Speak directly to that person. If you're angry, allow yourself to experience your anger by making a fist. Say, "I am angry. I am angry. I am angry. I am angry that ____." Finish the statement.

If you're scared, say, "I am scared, I am scared. I am scared. I am so scared that ____." Finish the statement.

If you are sad, say, "I am sad, I am sad. I am so sad. I am so sad that ____." Finish the statement.

After you've expressed your feelings, take two deep breaths. Are you ready to change the scene? If you are, then know you have the power to create it exactly as you want it to be.

So see things happening in front of you just the way you would have liked them to happen. What are you seeing? How are you feeling? What positive decision are you making?

Take two deep breaths and open your eyes. Write down your new positive thought. For example: Old fear, "I am so scared that I will always be alone." Affirm, "I, Your Name, am beginning to believe that there are people who want to be with me."

EXERCISE 5: SPRING CLEANING

Things that we have accumulated over the years sometimes keep us stuck in the past. They can make us feel heavy and cluttered. In order to let new things into our lives, we first have to make room by clearing out the old.

Go through your closets, drawers, cabinets and garage, whereever you've accumulated things that you don't need anymore. Get rid of the stuff in any way that feels good. Give it to your favorite charity, or sell it at a garage sale or flea market. If the mood strikes you, burn it. When you've completed this task, make an affirmation: "I am creating space for new things to come into my life."

EXERCISE 6: GIVING UP AN OLD FEAR

We need to uncover our out-of-date, unrealistic fears before we can give them up. The following exercise may help you change some of your misconceptions about success.

Close your eyes, breathe deeply and relax. See yourself successful in whatever you want to be. If it's a relationship, picture yourself in a loving relationship. If it's a job, see yourself in a stimulating, challenging job. How do you look?

Now, finish this sentence: "In order to create what I want, I am willing to give up the fear that ____."

Take two deep breaths and open your eyes. If you're ready to give up that negative thought, write it down on a piece of paper and throw it out or burn it. Then make an affirmation to replace that thought. For example: Burn, "I am ugly." Affirm, "I, Your Name, am beginning to believe that I am nice looking." Burn, "I am dumb." Affirm, "I, Your Name, am beginning to believe I am smart enough."

EXERCISE 7:   GIVING UP AN OLD IMAGE
If your image of yourself doesn't match what you want to become, you may end up sabotaging yourself. So let's work on creating a more positive picture.

Close your eyes and take two deep breaths. See an image of yourself in front of you. How do you look? Do you want to change your image?

If you do, then create a new image of yourself just the way you want to be. If you saw yourself as ugly, see yourself now as attractive. If you looked poor, see yourself as prosperous.

Take two deep breaths and open your eyes. Make an affirmation of your new image. "I, Your Name, am prosperous." Continue regularly to visualize your new image and repeat your affirmation aloud. To further reinforce it, you might also want to write it down.

EXERCISE 8:   YOU DO DESERVE SUCCESS
Everyone deserves success; it's our birthright. This exercise will help you find out what thoughts are telling you otherwise.

Write down on top of a piece of paper, "I deserve success because ____" and list the thoughts that come to mind.

Then write, "I don't deserve success because ____" and list your thoughts and feelings. If you have negative thoughts, change them with positive affirmations.

For example: Your negative thought might be, "I didn't work hard enough in school." Your affirmation, "I, Your Name, am beginning to accept that I did the best I could in school."

EXERCISE 9:   NOT GUILTY
Guilt feelings keep us stuck, making us believe that we're bad and don't deserve success. Your job is to clear out all the old guilt feelings so that you can feel good and allow yourself success and happiness.

Close your eyes and relax. Allow yourself to see the person you feel you have wronged, hurt or disappointed. He or she is standing in front of you right now. Admit what you did and ask for forgiveness. Picture this person forgiving you. Accept the forgiveness, and say, "I am okay and so are you." Take two deep breaths and open your eyes. Make an affirmation, "I, Your Name, am okay. '

EXERCISE 10: LET IT GO

If your guilt feelings continue to keep you stuck, write on a piece of paper, "I am bad because ____" or "I feel guilty because ____."

Then work on forgiving yourself and others in the following three ways:

1.   Write an apology to the person, even if he's already deceased. Mail it or throw it away.
2.   Write a note of forgiveness to yourself.
3.   Affirm, "I, Your Name, am a human being. I, Your Name, learn from my mistakes. I, Your Name, am a good person and I deserve success."

EXERCISE 11: SKYWRITING

If success has negative connotations attached to it, we tend to push it away. Sometimes, it's helpful actually to "see" the word "success" in order to uncover what it really means to you.

Close your eyes, breathe deeply and relax. Allow yourself to see the word "success" written in the sky.

Say, "Success means to me ____" and complete the sentence.

When you come up with a negative statement, go back to the time you decided that. Experience the old scene, express all your feelings.

When you're finished, change the scene to a more positive one and make an affirmation.

Take two deep breaths, open your eyes and write down your affirmation. You can repeat this exercise three more times, substituting the word "success" with "relationship," "money," "men" or "women."

For example: Say, "Success means to me responsibility.'' Now affirm, "I, Your Name, am successful and I can handle the responsibility."

EXERCISE 12: I CAN'T, I WON'T, I WILL

When you say "I can't," you feel powerless to do anything about your situation. But the truth is you're really very powerful: You CAN do many things you want to do. Maybe you just WON'T. By changing the statement "I can't" to "I won't," you reclaim your personal power. At that point, you have a choice, and you can change "I won't" to "I will."

On one piece of paper write, "I can't be successful because _____." List all your reasons. On another sheet of paper write, "I won't be successful because _____." Again, list your reasons.

These are the negative thoughts that are keeping you stuck. So, on a third sheet of paper, make an affirmation for each negative thought. For example: Write, "I can't be successful because I am a woman." Affirm, "I, Your Name, am beginning to believe I am a successful woman." Write, "I won't be successful because my friends won't like me." Affirm, "I, Your Name, am successful and my friends like me." Now, throw out the two pieces of paper with all your negative thoughts. Keep only your affirmations.

EXERCISE 13: MONEY AND YOU

Success often includes an abundance of money. But if you have unresolved issues about it, you are likely to push it away. It's necessary to feel good about money in order to allow prosperity into your life.

Close your eyes, take two complete breaths and relax. See money in front of you. What are you seeing? How do you feel? Tell the money that you deserve it.

If you don't believe that you do, go back to the time that you first made that decision. Re-live the experience, release the emotions, change the scene to a positive one, and make an affirmation.

Open your eyes and write down your affirmation. For example: Say, "I don't deserve money because I didn't work hard enough." Affirm, "I, Your Name, did the best I could and I deserve money."

EXERCISE 14: PRETTY MONEY

Money is no more than a piece of paper. There's nothing inherently bad about it, yet it's often associated with evil. This exercise will help you put money into its proper perspective.

Sit down with a pencil and paper and a real dollar bill. Look at the money closely, and complete this sentence, 'I see _____ and I feel _____."

Repeat it ten times and write down your answers. Now, look at what you've written. Notice any negative beliefs or feelings that you have about money; change them by making affirmations.

For example: Say, "I see a dirty piece of paper and I feel disgusted." Affirm, "I, Your Name, am beginning to believe that money is clean and I appreciate it."

At this point, you may have noticed how pretty money really is. Only people can make it evil, bad, or ugly.

EXERCISE 15: THE GIFT OF RECEIVING

Many people have trouble accepting gifts. This exercise will help you feel more comfortable receiving them.

Have a friend hand you a gift, and say to you, "Here is a gift. You deserve it."

How do you feel? If you don't feel that you deserve it, write on a piece of paper, "I don't want this gift because _____." Change your negative thoughts by making affirmations. For example: Say, "I don't deserve this gift because I am bad." Now affirm, 'I, Your Name, deserve this gift because I am a good person." Say, "I don't want this gift because then I will feel obligated to you." Affirm, "I, Your Name, accept this gift unconditionally."

EXERCISE 16: MOMMY AND DADDY, MAY I?

Unconsciously, we may push success away because we're afraid to be more successful than our parents. We need to believe that our parents want us to succeed.

Close your eyes and see your parents in front of you. Ask them if you can be successful and happy, if you can get what you want out of life. Hear them tell you that you can. Ask if they will still love you if you're more successful than they. Hear them say, "Yes."

If either or both parents give you a negative answer, then visualize a new set of nurturing parents who will support you. Hear them say the words you want to hear from them. End with an affirmation: "I, Your Name, am successful, and my parents love me."

Take two deep breaths, open your eyes and write down your affirmation.

EXERCISE 17: I'M ANGRY AT MY PARENTS

If you're angry at your parents and they wanted you to be successful, you may be spiting them by failing. You might be hurting them, but you're also hurting yourself. In order to change your pattern, you need to release your anger in a constructive way.

Put a pillow in front of you on your bed or in another safe place. Close your eyes and imagine that your father is in front of you. Tell him, "I am angry at you." Yell at him. If you're concerned about the noise, scream into the pillow. Also make a fist and pound the pillow until your anger is spent. Do the same with your mother.

Finally, tell your parents, "I will be successful because I choose to be."

Take two deep breaths, open your eyes and make an affirmation: "I, Your Name, am successful in my career/relationships because I want to be."

EXERCISE 18: GOING FOR WHAT I WANT AND DESERVE

Fears can paralyze us. In this exercise, you will face your worst fears and probably discover that they're not nearly as scary as you first believed.

Write down on a piece of paper, "I want to _____, and I won't because _____." Finish the sentence.

Now ask yourself, "What is the worst thing that could happen if I go for it? What is worse than that? And worse than that?" Continue until you uncover the absolute worst thing.

When you're finished, you might discover that the only thing worse than going for what you want is staying where you are. Make an affirmation.

For example: "I want to quit my job, but I won't because I'm afraid to give up the security. If I quit my job, the worst thing that can happen is that I won't be able to find a new job. Even worse, I might fail in a new job. But even worse than that is being stuck in the miserable job I have now. So, I, Your Name, want to try a new career, and I am going for it."

EXERCISE 19: MOVING BEYOND

Many people are afraid that if they are successful, others will resent them. The following can help you get a new perspective concerning this fear.

Close your eyes and relax. See the people in front of you who do not want you to be successful or who are jealous of your success. You might see your parents, siblings, friends or co-workers.

Tell them, "I am sorry that you are stuck. I am moving on to create what I want in my life. And I am meeting people who support my success. I want you to know that when you're ready, you can be successful, too. I am giving you a gift by modeling success for you."

EXERCISE 20: FINISH OLD BUSINESS

Unfinished business keeps us stuck, so it's important that we clear it up. If you want to stop this exercise at any time, feel free to go to your safe place. If you feel scared, imagine that your wise person is with you.

Lie down on a mattress or have pillows on either side of you. Close your eyes, breathe deeply and relax. Allow yourself to visualize someone with whom you're angry. It may be your mother, father, sister, brother, teacher, boss, or child, or anyone in your present or past.

See that person in front of you and tell them that you're angry. There are no consequences, because you're really all by yourself. You may want to hit a pillow or yell into a pillow. Say or yell whatever you want to say to that person.

When you've exhausted your anger, tell that person that you forgive him for what he did. Say, "I forgive you. I, Your Name, am okay and so are you."

Take two big breaths, open your eyes and write down your affirmation.

EXERCISE 21: IT'S YOUR TURN NOW

If you're angry at yourself for mistakes you made in the past, you may still be punishing yourself. In order to allow yourself to feel good, you need to release the anger and forgive yourself.

As above, have pillows next to you. Close your eyes and take two deep breaths. See an image of yourself standing in front of you. Get in touch with some reason that you're punishing yourself. Tell yourself why this makes you so angry. Say, "I am angry at you because _____."

For example, "I am angry at you because you don't work hard enough."

Get all the anger out by yelling and pounding on your pillow. When your anger subsides, make an affirmation: "I, Your Name, forgive myself, and I am okay."

Take two deep breaths, open your eyes and repeat your affirmation.

EXERCISE 22: INNER POWER AND THE TOP OF THE MOUNTAIN

People climb mountains all the time. Although they may say they do it simply because the mountains are there, the truth is that they feel a tremendous sense of accomplishment and power when they reach the top. The following can help you experience that same kind of inner power.

Close your eyes and take two deep breaths. Imagine that you're in a meadow and you see a beautiful mountain in front of you. Allow yourself to climb effortlessly to the top of that mountain.

What are you seeing? How are you feeling? Breathe in all that clean, fresh air. When you're ready, slowly return to the meadow, open your eyes and write down an affirmation. For example, "I, Your Name, am feeling peacefully powerful."

EXERCISE 23: SHARE YOUR MOUNTAIN

Sharing your mountain with someone special intensifies your good feelings for him or her and makes you feel even closer. Close your eyes and take two deep breaths. Imagine that you've returned to the meadow with a person you feel good about. It must be someone with whom you have already cleared up any unfinished business. It may be one of your parents, your spouse, children, or even your wise person.

Ask that person if he wants to climb the mountain with you. If he does, then see the mountain in front of you. Imagine that you and the other person are effortlessly climbing or flying to the top of the mountain together. Experience the beauty, calmness and inner peace.

When you're ready to leave, return to the meadow. Take two deep breaths and open your eyes. Make an affirmation. For example, "I, Your Name, and my spouse are experiencing our inner peace and power."

EXERCISE 24: FLIGHT PLAN TO SUCCESS

To reinforce your visualizations and affirmations, you may be ready to make your own flight plan to success. A flight plan is a drawing or collage depicting your specific goals, showing your life as you would like it to be. Transferring your definition of success into a physical drawing will help you clarify more fully what you want out of life. And clarifying your specific wants is a powerful step in attaining them.

Before you begin your flight plan, you may want to picture it by doing the following visual exercise: Close your eyes, take two deep breaths and see yourself successful and happy in a life exactly like you want it to be. Where are you? How do you look? What are you doing? Who are you with? What is your life like?

When you feel your picture is complete, take two deep breaths, open your eyes and begin putting your visualizations down on a piece of paper or posterboard. Use lots of colorful crayons or felt pens. If you want, use actual photographs or pictures you cut from newspapers or magazines. Under each picture, write the appropriate affirmation.

Be specific. If you want to be thin, make sure the picture of you is thin. If you want to be in a fulfilling job, put yourself in the picture just the way you envision it. If your goal is to find the ideal relationship, show the man or woman of your dreams. If you plan to buy a new car, be certain that your picture or drawing is the exact one you want, right down to the color.

I have found that we actualize what we visualize. So make sure that your flight plan is an accurate representation of your dreams and desires. Now hang it someplace where you can refer to it frequently.

You will know that you've broken through your Fear of Success as soon as you begin reaching the goals on your flight plan. If, however, you're not accomplishing them, you have some more work to do. First, re-evaluate your wants to see if they have changed. If not, your subconscious Fear of Success might still be sabotaging you. In that case, repeat some of the previous success exercises.

EXERCISE 25: GO FOR IT

It's important to like and love yourself in order to allow yourself to feel happy and successful.

Hold a soft, cuddly pillow or stuffed animal in your arms. Close your eyes and relax. Imagine that the pillow or stuffed animal is you, and hold it close.

Say to yourself: "You, Your Name, are okay. You are a good person. I like you. I love you. You deserve success and happiness."

You really do deserve it! We all do. Go for it!

And now you have the tools to move past the fears that were blocking you. With them, you can achieve your goals and desires, and experience that internal feeling of fulfillment, peace and power which comes from being who you really are and doing what you truly want to do.

It might interest you to know that while I was writing this book, I was also working with the tools. Although I was already a successful therapist, lecturer and director of my own institute, I had trouble picturing myself as a successful author. For one thing, it didn't fit my image of myself. For another, I felt overwhelmed by the opportunities it would open up for me.

I had to overcome these fears before I would allow myself to finish this book and get it published. And now that I have, I am looking forward to new challenges and achievements.

As you can see, successful people don't stay in one place; success leads to success. And each new level of accomplishment can bring with it new fears.

As you begin to move on, you may face new fears and start sabotaging yourself again. When you do, review the techniques in this book in order to move beyond your Fear of Success and be *Free To Fly!*

Appendix

ADDITIONAL TOOLS THAT CLIENTS USE TO FEEL
HAPPIER, HEALTHIER, AND MORE SUCCESSFUL

COMMUNICATING WITH YOURSELF

I. **S.O.S. (HELP — I feel bad, angry, scared, etc.)**
"WHAT AM I TELLING MYSELF?"
   1. "The event = I am not okay."
   2. "The event = The event."
   3. "I am okay."

   EXAMPLE
   1. "My boss yelled at me = I am not okay."
   2. "My boss yelled at me = My boss yelled at me."
   3. "I am okay."

II. **CAN'T/WON'T**
"I can't lose weight."
"I won't lose weight."
(You may change it to, "I will lose weight.")

III. **GUILT/RESENTMENT**
If you feel guilty, say, "I *should. . . .*" or *"I am not okay."*
Then say, "I resent. . . ." (the other side of guilt)
Finally, say "I want to. . . . and I am okay."

   EXAMPLE
   "I feel guilty when I come late. I should always be on time or I am not okay. I resent always having to be on time. I want to be on time, or I am okay when I am late."

IV. **THINK/FEEL**
To find out what is really going on with you, check out your thoughts and feelings. They are two separate parts. Ask yourself, "What am I *thinking?*" or "What do I *know?*" (*Mind*) and "What am I *feeling?*" or "What am I *experiencing?*" (*Body*).

V. INTUITION

Another reliable source of information for you is your sixth sense or intuition. It is the psychic, perceptive part of you which is picking up signals for no obvious reasons. Trust your intuition. It is a very valuable part of you. Ask yourself, "What am I *sensing?*" or allow yourself to close your eyes and see your wise person. Ask him/her a question and be your wise person and answer it.

COMMUNICATING WITH OTHERS

I. POSITIVE/NEGATIVE REQUESTS

Rather than a negative "Don't yell at me!", use a positive "I would like you to calmly tell me what you want."

II. I WANT/YOU SHOULD

The most powerful form of communication is "I want. . .," or "I would like. . .," or "I prefer. . .," because people want clear messages. This expands communication, which makes it easier for others to give you what you want. To say "You should. . .," or "Why did you. . .," or "Don't you think. . . ," will close down communication and make it difficult for you to get what you want.

III. COMMUNICATION/NON-COMMUNICATION

If someone is not communicating with you, you may be doing one or more of the following:
1. Not listening
2. Judging
3. Talking too much
4. Interrupting
5. Not being interested in the other person's communication
6. Not being patient
7. Criticizing
8. Being sarcastic
9. Overreacting
10. Psychoanalyzing
11. Labeling
12. Cursing

To encourage communication, use these tools:
1. To let the other person know that you are listening, use eye contact, nod, or say, Uh-huh."
2. Really listen, avoid thinking of what to say next, and give

feedback by repeating what the other person said in your own words.

3. Talk less. Ask, "What are you thinking? How are you feeling? What is your opinion? How was your day?"
4. Allow the other person to finish speaking.
5. If the other person's chosen topic is not interesting to you, tell him, "I hear you and I would rather talk about. . . Is that okay with you?"
6. Be patient.
7. Accept others' communications as statements of themselves. There is no right or wrong, just different opinions and feelings. *Communication is sharing your thoughts and feelings.*
8. Avoid proving right or wrong by communicating statements of what you are thinking and feeling.
9. Accept what the other person is saying in the now. Recognize that people change.
10. Express your enjoyment of communicating and sharing yourself, and how much you appreciate the other person's communication with you.

IV. **ENHANCING COMMUNICATIONS:**

Say:	**Avoid:**
1. I imagine. . .	I know. . .
2. I like you and. . .	I like you but. . .
3. I feel. . .	You feel. . .
4. What are you feeling?	Why are you feeling. . .?
5. How are you feeling?	Why are you feeling. . .?
6. Sometimes, I notice you. . .	You always. . .
7. Often, I notice you. . .	You never. . .
8. I resent. . .	You make me. . .
9. What do you think?	Don't you think. . .?
10. I would like you to. . .	You should. . .

V. **MORE GUIDELINES:**
1. Take time to communicate with yourself; tune into your own thoughts and feelings to be clearly aware of what you want to communicate to others.
2. Take responsibility; begin your sentences with, "I. . . ."
3. Follow "I feel. . ." with a feeling; "I feel sad."
4. Follow "I think. . ." with a thought: "I think that you are mindreading."
5. Make a statement rather than ask a question.
6. Avoid mindreading; if you are unclear about any communication, ask for specifics: "How do you mean that?

126

What do you mean?"

7. Watch for non-verbal messages: gestures, posture, tone of voice, etc.

8. Rather than giving advice, point out the different choices you see and allow the other person to decide.

VI. COMMUNICATION CONTRACT:

"I care about you and I want you to communicate with me. I would like you to trust me with your thoughts and feelings. I don't want to judge you, interrupt you, advise you, nor to try to solve your problems. I want to listen to you and be really present for you. I want the same gift from you. It is such a joy to communicate with you and maintain the bridge between us so we can be close. I feel so good being close to you!"

HOW TO CLEAR UNFINISHED BUSINESS

1. Clearing unfinished business is a gift to you and others. When we do not clear resentments, we act them out through active or passive aggression. That behavior hurts us as well as the other person.

2. Right Brain Process: If you feel angry or upset with a person, then imagine that they are on a pillow and release all your feelings. (Remember that you are responsible for all your feelings.)

3. Left Brain Process: Then when you are calm and centered, fill out the following:

    a) "I have a problem when you _____."
       (specific event)

       or

       "I feel _____, when you _____."
          (feeling)   (specific event)

    b) "I would like you to _____."
                         (specific request)

4. Now, either write the above statements (a) and (b) to the person, or contact them to make an appointment in order to clear the issue.

5. Example:

    a) "I have a gift for you." Or, "I would like to work with you so I want to clear an issue." Or, "I care about you so I want to clear unfinished business with you." (Introduction)

    b) "I have a problem, when you come late to meetings."
       or

128

"I feel resentful, when you come late to meetings."

c)   "I would like you to come to meetings on time."

d)   "Are you willing to come to meetings on time?"

e)   "Thank you for helping me clear with you." (Closure)

DEALING WITH ANGER

Many people are joyously singing "LET THERE BE PEACE ON EARTH AND LET IT BEGIN WITH ME." I love that song and I totally believe in what it is telling us. I am convinced that when we human beings who inhabit this world experience inner peace, then, and only then will we actualize long-lasting world peace.

I used to feel so powerless when I read the horrible stories in the newspaper. However, I realized how powerful I was to affect the world, when I focused on changing myself and helping others to grow also. I became aware of the inner turmoil in myself and others that was preventing us from feeling peacefully powerful. So, I kept exploring what we needed to do in order to end our internal wars and experience inner peace.

As a growing person and a psychotherapist, I have found that one important thing we have to learn in order to experience inner peace is how to deal with our own personal anger. This human emotion is often denied, misunderstood and misused. And, I have discovered that it is dangerous for us and the world when we don't deal constructively with our anger. I would like to share with you what I have learned about dealing with anger.

1. What is anger?
    Anger is a normal, healthy human emotion. And, it is important to understand that whenever you are feeling angry, you are also feeling some underlying emotions, too. These other feelings are: fear, hurt and a sense of powerlessness. Therefore, when you deal with your anger you also need to deal with all the underlying emotions.

2. Where in your body do you feel anger?
    Most people feel anger in the form of tension or pain in their forehead, jaws, cheeks, temples, arms, hands, center of the back of the neck, and the back (especially the shoulder blades and the lower back).

3. What are some physical problems or illnesses that may result from suppressed anger?
Some physical problems that may indicate anger is present are: headaches; jaw, gum and teeth problems (from grinding the teeth); arthritis in the fingers or hands; back problems; stroke and heart attack ("I am busting a gut"); high blood pressure ("I am boiling"); bursitis in the shoulder ("I want to hit someone"); constipation and extreme tiredness. (Note: Depression is anger turned inwards. When you release your anger in a constructive way, your depression may also be released.)

4. Is anger a good (positive) or bad (negative) emotion?
Anger is one of many emotions (feelings). Emotions are not good or bad, positive or negative. They are feelings that have to be expressed. People have the choice of dealing with anger in a positive or negative way (constructive or destructive).

5. How do people express anger in a negative way?
Some people act out their anger in what is called ACTIVE AGGRESSION. And others act it out in PASSIVE AGGRESSION. And some people alternate between active and passive aggression.

ACTIVE AGGRESSORS may shout, curse, or physically attack a person or a thing. Some examples are: hitting, rape, murder, starting fires, and defacing property.

PASSIVE AGGRESSORS may quietly withdraw, be late, be sarcastic, procrastinate, forget important dates, verbally attack with a soft voice and a smile, or overeat.

6. Does physical activity help release anger?
Physical activity helps relieve some of the angry energy that results from angry feelings, but it does not RESOLVE the anger. Therefore, the angry feelings still present will create more angry energy, and you have to keep running faster or hitting the ball harder in order to keep from exploding.

7. Why do most people deny or resist accepting their angry feelings?
Most people block their anger because they are afraid that if they are angry, then they will:
   1. hurt someone else or themselves
   2. be hurt by someone else
   3. be out of control or crazy

131

4. be wasting their time ("I don't accomplish anything, so why bother?)
5. be bad or not okay
6. be unlady-like
7. be rejected
8. be like their parent and they hated when their parent was angry
9. be too powerful
10. be giving their power to the other person ("The other person will know they won or got to me.")

8. How can I deal with my anger in a positive way?
    You can deal with your anger in a constructive way by first acknowledging it. Then, by yourself or with someone you trust, imagine that the person you are angry at is on a soft pillow, and angrily yell and hit the pillow until your anger is released. After that, get in touch with an underlying feeling which may be fear, hurt, or powerlessness. After you have owned and expressed all your feelings, then make an affirmation. For example:
    1. If you are angry when Gene comes home late, then imagine he/she is on a pillow and release your angry feelings.
    2. Then say to yourself, "When you are late, I am scared that I am unimportant."
    3. Affirmation: "I, Your Name, am beginning to believe that I am important."
    4. Now, if you are feeling calm because you understand your feelings and have released them, decide if you need or want to talk to the person about the issue of coming late in person, by letter, or by telephone.
    5. And, finally, compliment yourself for dealing with your anger in a healthy, positive and constructive way. REWARD YOURSELF! YOU DESERVE IT!

BALANCING YOUR LIFE

In order to be a whole person, feel good and avoid burn-out, we need to balance our lives. Basically, we have four parts: physical, mental, emotional and spiritual. All of our parts are important and valuable. They all need acceptance, appreciation and time to be expressed.

The following outline can help you balance your life:

1.   First, look at your year. What are your goals in each area of your life? (Goals need to be specific, measurable, attainable and truly things you desire.) Ask yourself:
   a)   What are your relationship or social goals?
   b)   What are your professional goals?
   c)   What are your financial goals?
   d)   When and where do you want to go on vacations?
   e)   How do you want your physical body to be and what programs are you going to participate in to achieve your goals?
   f)   What do you want to focus on learning this year? (mental)
   g)   How do you want to grow emotionally?
   h)   How are you going to grow spiritually?
   i)   What are your goals with your family?
   j)   How are you going to have fun and play?

2.   Then, get a monthly calendar. Set your goals for the month and begin to balance your month. For example, schedule: a weekend a month to go away; one day of the week or half a day to have "alone" time; working hours, and classes and responsibilities. Now look at the whole picture. Does it look balanced?

3.   Then, get a weekly calendar and schedule and balance your week.

4. Finally, have a daily calendar and look at your day. Check out if it is balanced. Have you included all your parts (physical, mental, emotional and spiritual). Ask yourself, when am I:

_____1. Working?

_____2. Playing?

_____3. Exercising?

_____4. Meditating?

_____5. Eating properly?

_____6. Resting?

_____7. Saying or writing my affirmations (positive thoughts)?

HOW TO NURTURE YOURSELF

1. Take a bubble bath
2. Buy yourself a rose(s)
3. Take a sauna
4. Get a massage
5. Take a bath by candlelight
6. Have breakfast in bed
7. Go to the pet store and play with the animals
8. Visit the zoo
9. Walk on a scenic path
10. Stop and smell the flowers
11. Have a manicure or pedicure
12. Wake up early and watch the sunrise
13. Watch the sunset
14. Relax with a good book and/or soothing music
15. Light the fireplace for yourself
16. Play your favorite music and dance to it by yourself
17. Go to bed early
18. Sleep outside under the stars
19. Stay in bed all day when you're well
20. Fix a special dinner just for you and eat by candlelight
21. Participate in your favorite sport
22. Go for a walk
23. Take a walk in the rain
24. Run on the beach
25. Take a scenic drive
26. Meditate
27. Buy new underpants
28. Browse in a book or record store for as long as you want
29. Buy yourself a cuddly stuffed animal
30. Write yourself a love letter and mail it
31. Ask a special person to nurture you (feed, cuddle, and/or read to you)
32. Buy yourself something special that you can afford

33. Go see a good film or show
34. Go to the park and feed the ducks, swing on the swings, etc.
35. Visit a museum or other interesting place
36. Go to the harbor and listen to the boats
37. Have a facial
38. Give yourself a facial
39. Go into a hot tub or Jacuzzi
40. Record an affirmation tape
41. Make a flight plan for success
42. Call an old friend
43. Bake or cook something special
44. Go window shopping
45. Buy a meditation tape
46. Listen to a positive, motivation tape
47. Write in your special book all your wins for the day
48. Gently apply a fragrant lotion all over your body
49. Masturbate
50. Tell yourself all the things you appreciate and love about you, and give yourself a big hug.

BE SELF-CARING! NURTURE YOURSELF EVERYDAY!

YOU NEED IT AND YOU DESERVE IT!

HOW TO NURTURE YOURSELF BY GIVING AND RECEIVING

When you unconditionally give to others, you are giving for the enjoyment of giving. When you unconditionally receive from others, you allow them the gift of giving. The following are some suggestions of how to nurture yourself by giving and receiving:

Receiving

Ask someone to:
1. serve you breakfast in bed
2. massage you
3. be your chauffeur for a period of time
4. work with you on a project (hobby, chore, etc.)
5. make all the plans for a date and surprise you
6. take pictures of you as you pose
7. feed you
8. wash your back, hair, or all of you
9. call you and say something nice on your answering machine
10. do something nice for you
11. take you away for a day or a weekend
12. treat you to a meal and/or a show

Giving

1. send a nice card or letter
2. tell people what you appreciate about them
3. give a present (for no specific reason)
4. bring or send flowers
5. treat someone to a meal and/or a show
6. pay the toll for the car behind you
7. send money to charity
8. volunteer your time where needed
9. become a Big Sister or Big Brother

10. be friendly to someone who is lonely
11. invite a lonely person to your party
12. call someone from your past
13. give a massage
14. serve someone breakfast in bed
15. do a good deed

BE SELF CARING! NURTURE YOURSELF EVERYDAY!

YOU NEED IT AND DESERVE IT!

SEVEN KEYS TO A GREAT RELATIONSHIP

1. I am ready to create what I want in a relationship.

2. I am my own best friend and I am responsible for my own life and happiness.

3. I am learning to communicate clearly, specifically and constructively.

4. I am letting go of hurtful thoughts and feelings from my past relationships.

5. I am continually seeking excitement, fun and the magic of life with my partner.

6. I am allowing myself and my partner to explore and develop our individual potentials.

7. I am loving and accepting my partner unconditionally.

SUGGESTED READING

There are many wonderful books out there to assist you in your growth process. Some of them are:

Creative Visualization by Shakti Gawain. Whatever Publishing, 1978.

Handbook to Higher Consciousness by Ken Keys, Jr. Living Love Publishing, 1975.

I Deserve Love by Sondra Ray. Les Femmes, 1976.

Peoplemaking by Virginia Satir. Science and Behavior Books, Inc. 1972.

Making Contact by Virginia Satir. Celestial Arts, 1976.

Bioenergetics by Alexander Lowen, M.D. Penguin Books, 1975.

Psychosynthesis by Robert Assagioli, M.D. Penguin Books, 1965.

The Prophet by Kahlil Gibran. Alfred A. Knopf, 1923.

The Magical Child Within You by Bruce and Jenny Davis. Inner Light Books, 1983.

Gestalt Therapy Verbatim by Frederick S. Perls, M.D. Bantam Books, 1959.

The Transparent Self by Sidney M. Jourard. D. Van Nostrand Co., 1971.

The Intimate Enemy by George R. Bach and Peter Wyden. Avon Books, 1968.

141

Born To Win by Muriel James and Dorothy Jongward. Addison-Wesley, 1971.

Getting Well Again by O. Carl Simonton, M.D., Stephanie Matthews-Simonton, and James L. Creighton. Bantam Books, 1978.

ABOUT THE INSTITUTE FOR CREATIVE THERAPY

The Institute for Creative Therapy, a non-profit educational center, is dedicated to helping people experience success and happiness in their lives.

The Institute offers:
Individual, Couple and Family Counseling in private and group sessions.

Workshops and Seminars on:
- Fears of Success
- Improving Relationships
- Stress Management
- Prosperity
- Dealing with Anger

- Weight Control
- Alcohol and Drug Addiction
- Successful Parenting
- Communication Skills
- Balancing Your Life
- And More. . .

Training and Internship — intensive training of counselors in Creative Therapy.

Speakers Program — members of the Institute are available for lectures.

Tapes Available:
Breaking Through Your Fear of Success, by Helene Rothschild. This tape will first help you identify the Seven Fears of Success that may be keeping you stuck and frustrated. Then you will be guided through powerful exercises designed to help you succeed in your relationships, career, prosperity, weight control, and other personal goals.

Dare To Be Thin!, by Helene Rothschild. Side one explores the fears that may be keeping you from achieving and maintaining your desired weight. Side two guides you through visual exercises to help you overcome your fears around weight loss so that you can win the "battle of the bulge".

I Deserve It All!, by Helene Rothschild. Helene will give you powerful affirmations which will help you create what you want in your life.

To order your tape(s), send your name, address and $14.00 each (postage and handling included) to the address below.

For further information or to receive notice of new tapes and upcoming workshops, contact:

HELENE ROTHSCHILD, DIRECTOR
INSTITUTE FOR CREATIVE THERAPY
P. O. BOX 31007
LOS GATOS, CALIFORNIA 95031-1601

ABOUT THE AUTHORS

Helene Rothschild was born and raised in Brooklyn, New York. She received a B.S. and M.S. Degree in Education from Brooklyn College. In 1976 she moved to California and studied at the University of Santa Clara where she earned an M.A. in Marriage, Family and Child Counseling.

While she was counseling clients as a licensed therapist, she began to develop her own theory and techniques which she calls Creative Therapy — a powerful, innovative process that allows people to release their emotional pain and negative beliefs that keep them from achieving success, and helps them take charge of their lives.

In June 1982, she founded and began directing the Institute for Creative Therapy, a non-profit educational center. At the Institute she trains and supervises interns in Creative Therapy, and counsels clients in private and group sessions.

Helene has facilitated over 200 workshops, lectured extensively and appeared on radio and television. For six months she hosted her own San Jose Cable TV show called, "Creative Therapy with Helene Rothschild".

She is well-known for her warmth, good humor and her inspiring speaking ability. She is often invited to be the motivational or keynote speaker at seminars and conferences. Helene's business card summarizes her belief:

You can create what you want in your life!

Marsha Kay Seff has been a magazine and newspaper writer for the last 15 years. She has written for such publications as the Miami Herald, Binghamton Press, San Jose Mercury-News, Riverside Press-Enterprise, Ft. Lauderdale News, Miami Beach Sun, Phoenix Republic, BusinessWoman Magazine, Essence Magazine and Venture Magazine. Born in Miami Beach, Florida, she is a graduate of the University of Florida. She is currently living in San Diego, California, where she is a reporter for the San Diego Union. Her hobbies include playing tennis and riding and breeding Peruvian Paso horses.